Corporate Growth and
Common Stock Risk

CONTEMPORARY STUDIES IN
ECONOMIC AND FINANCIAL ANALYSIS VOL. 12

Editors: Professor Edward I. Altman and Ingo Walter, Associate Dean
  Graduate School of Business Administration, New York University

CONTEMPORARY STUDIES IN ECONOMIC AND FINANCIAL ANALYSIS

An International Series of Monographs

Series Editors: Edward I. Altman and Ingo Walter

Graduate School of Business Administration, New York University

For Irene, Melanie and Natalie

Corporate Growth and Common Stock Risk

by **DAVID R. FEWINGS**
Faculty of Management
McGill University

Foreword by **MYRON GORDON**
University of Toronto

 **JAI PRESS INC.**

Greenwich, Connecticut

Library of Congress Cataloging in Publication Data

Fewings, David R
    Corporate growth and common stock risk.

    (Contemporary studies in economic and financial
analysis; v. 12)
    Includes bibliographical references and index.
    1. Corporations—Growth—Mathematical models.
2. Dividends—Mathematical models.   3.   Risk—
Mathematical models.   4.   Capital asset pricing
model.   5.   Corporations—Valuation—Mathematical
models.   I. Title.   II.   Series.
HG4011.F39   332.6'3223   76-52014
ISBN 0-89232-053-2

Contents

Tables

Foreword

In *The Investment Financing and Valuation of the Corporation* I hypothesized that the yield investors require on a corporation's shares is an increasing function of the expected rate of growth in the company's dividend. If true, the theorem has a profound influence on theory and practice in security valuation and the cost of capital.

The risk and pricing of growth stocks and the econometric analysis of cross section data on the pricing of common stocks provided strong empirical evidence in support of the theorem. However, empirical evidence is not enough. Confidence in a theorem and its use to advance knowledge are materially enhanced by a strong theoretical foundation. Unfortunately, throughout the sixties and early seventies every effort to establish that theoretical foundation met with failure.

It was therefore difficult for me to contain my excitement when it became evident that David Fewings had solved the problem. He shows in this book that under very weak assumptions the yield investors require on a share is an increasing function of the firm's *investment rate*—and not simply dividend growth, as I had hypothesized. Without doubt this is the most important contribution to the theory of security valuation and the cost of capital so far this decade.

Every important contribution to knowledge becomes obvious once it has been made. We always knew that long bonds tend to sell at higher yields than short bonds, and the holding period return risk of a bond increases with its maturity. If a stock is a very long bond we have it. However, a stock is not a bond. Among other things, the future payments as well as the future discount rates are uncertain.

Fewings solved the problem by joining my intrinsic value model, in which risk is consigned to a black box, with the Sharpe-Lintner-Mossin capital asset pricing model in which everything else is consigned to a black box. In addition, he does a masterful job of dealing with dividend policy and the informational content of the dividend.

The joining of the Gordon intrinsic value model and the SLM-CAPM will be the foundation for numerous other contributions to the theory of finance over the next decade. An appreciation and mastery of what has been accomplished here will be useful, if not necessary, reading for everyone who will be working in the area of security valuation and the cost of capital.

Myron J. Gordon

Preface

This book concerns the effect of expected corporate growth on the investment risk of common stocks. The research began during my doctoral studies at the University of Toronto when it became apparent to me that the effects of unexpected changes in capital market conditions, as reflected in changes in capitalization factors and profitability expectations, were not well understood by financial economists. For example, the process generating investment returns on common stocks was generally modeled in the literature only in terms of fluctuating cash flows to the corporations concerned. It was not generally recognized that much of the risk of investing in stocks arises from unexpected revisions in investor assessments of future profit potential or from changes in the general equilibrium rates of time preference, risk premium requirements, and inflation outlook. Of particular concern to me in light of this was the possibility of uncovering the basis for a dividend policy effect on stock valuation. This was something that was widely believed in but which had never been satisfactorily proven or disproven under conditions sufficiently general to allow for changing capitalization rates and profit potential assessments in addition to stochastic corporate cash flows. Alas, early analytical results confirmed the view that dividend policy, per se, has no effect on stock valuation in capital markets approaching conditions of perfect competition. However, the analysis also indicated that the rate at which a firm is expected to invest and achieve growth in earnings is a major factor in the determination of common stock risk, regardless of whether the required equity is obtained by retaining earnings or by issuing new stock. Subsequent empirical work in both Canada and the United States supports this finding which has profound implications, for both investors and corporate decision makers alike.

As a monograph dealing with one particular aspect of finance this book is not expected to find broad use as a student text. However, since it deals with an aspect of investment and corporate decision making which is central to the theory and practice of Finance, the book should prove interesting to officers of major corporations, to investment analysts interested in the relationships between corporate growth, stock risk and stock value, and to graduate students and professors of Finance studying aspects of investment financing and valuation of corporations.

In the course of preparing this research I have received the encouragement and assistance of many people. Among these, I wish to express my special gratitude to Myron J. Gordon, who gave me the benefit of his great insight and inspiring confidence. Paul Halpern and James Pesando deserve thanks for serving with Mike on my dissertation committee, and Martin Gruber has my thanks for his contribution and encouragement as an outside reader at that stage of the development. Ed Altman has provided valuable guidance in his role as Associate Editor of this series. Cheryl Karas deserves much credit and has my gratitude for typing the manuscript. Finally, a very special and heartfelt thanks to my wife, Irene.

Chapter I

Introduction

The development of capital asset pricing theory, an equilibrium model of the relationship between the expected return on assets and an operational measure of the contribution of individual assets to the risk of portfolios, has contributed immensely to financial theory as a useful fund of knowledge. Prior to capital asset pricing theory, however, a large body of useful literature on dividend valuation evolved which has served to sharpen the issues of corporate finance. More sophisticated than the capital asset pricing model in terms of relating to fundamental corporate variables such as leverage, earnings retention, stock financing rates, return on assets, and return on equity investments; these dividend valuation models relate closely to the characteristics of individual firms but have very limited potential for providing insights with respect to the implications of uncertainty and risk aversion. This is due to their partial equilibrium nature and consequent reliance upon a summary measure of the effect of uncertainty and risk aversion, such as a risk adjustment in the discount rate or, equivalently, certain equivalent factors for uncertain future receipts. Therefore, on one hand we have a model of general equilibrium risk and return which is operationally powerful in dealing with the phenomena of uncertainty in investments and risk averse investors, and on the other we have models of share valuation in partial equilibrium which are relatively sophisticated in modeling stock valuation in terms of corporate characteristics including those associated with various definitions of corporate growth. In this book we make use of both types of models jointly in order to study the effects of corporate growth on the risk of investing in common stocks.

Joint use has been made of the general equilibrium capital asset pricing model and intrinsic valuation models in the past to study capital budgeting criteria and the effects of leverage and regulation of systematic risk.[1] There has also been a study published which investigates stock risk in terms of earnings or cash-flow risk, and risk that stems from changing capitalization rates.[2] However, such studies have consistently avoided the use of valuation models which allow for corporate growth in favor of simpler models which assume that future income receipts have stationary distributions. The expectation of capital gains or losses has typically been handled by defining the future flows in terms of a perpetuity-equivalent stream or by defining a separate stochastic capital gain variable for the purpose. However, this effectively assumes away the whole growth expectation problem, with the consequence that the resulting analytical outcome provides no insights concerning the effects of growth. In order to avoid that problem we employ valuation models that are specifically oriented to study the determinants and effects of growth, and which have been widely published in connection with the controversy concerning the effects of dividend policy.

That there are problems involved in using the single period capital asset pricing model implicitly as a multi-period valuation model has been determined by Merton[3] and others. For investor utility of wealth functions other than the logarithmic one first proposed by Bernoulli in 1738, it may be the case that a modification of the single period capital asset pricing model's measure of undiversifiable risk is required to take into account complications in optimal portfolio choice that arise because of correlation that exists between changes in market equilibrium capitalization rates which impact on holding period returns and changes in the investment opportunities available at the end of holding periods. However, in order to avoid the extremely complex, and seemingly intractable, analysis which arises when studying the effects of corporate growth on common stock risk in the context of the intertemporal capital asset pricing model, it will be assumed that the measure of common stock risk derived in the single period model is adequate for our purposes. It is believed that the insight to be gained by studying the implications of corporate growth for common stock risk is worth the cost of this type of assumption in terms of the resulting lack of absolute rigor in the analysis. Whether or not the conclusions to be reached are sufficiently robust to withstand further analytical inquiry is a question that can be answered to some extent by considering the nature of the insight gained and by examining empirical evidence on the importance of the effects discovered.

CONSIDERATION OF CORPORATE GROWTH AND CLASSIFICATION OF RISK SOURCES

Of the factors which affect the risk of investing in common stocks, the most widely agreed upon include the type of business in which the corporation is engaged, the extent to which operating leverage is employed, and the degree to which the common equity is levered by the use of debt and preferred equity financing. Although high risk is frequently attributed to the common stock of firms with high real investment rate objectives, the nature of the causal relationship between real investment rates and common stock risk is not as clearly understood as the more obvious link between financial leverage and risk, for example. Nevertheless, the rate of growth to which corporations are committed for various reasons is perhaps one of the most important factors determining the risk of investing in common stocks. This book is concerned with the causal nature of this growth-risk relationship, and with the empirical importance of the relationship in both an absolute and relative sense. In order to facilitate the study it is necessary to consider a classification of the sources of stock risk at a level suitable to the analysis of growth effects. The effect of corporate growth on risk from each source can then be examined in more detail.

One source of common stockholder risk, and the one most often referred to directly, is uncertainty concerning the earnings to be realized on existing common equity investments during the holding period of the investor. If we think, for the present, strictly in terms of the effect on stockholder wealth of a transitory departure of earnings or cash flow from what is expected in a given period, the effect is a relatively small one. For example, if a stock is trading at ten times expected earnings, and if actual earnings (and cash flow) realized fall short of the expectation by 10 percent for some entirely transitory reason, the firm's shareholders will be approximately 1 percent worse off than expected. The effect on shareholder wealth is so small in this case because we have, for expositional purposes, specified the shortfall as being entirely transitory and, although it is 10 percent of expected earnings, the decline in profit receipts is a much smaller fraction of the value of common stock. We assume the latter continues to trade at ten times expected future earnings.

Of course, if the long-run future profitability of the firm is reassessed by the market, the effect on holding period return to investors is much more significant than that caused by a transitory departure of earnings from expected levels. The risk of such a reassessment of long-run profit rate expectations by the market can be thought of as a second source of investment risk because, although such reassessments are frequently contemporaneous with unanticipated earnings outcomes, very often they are completely independent of earnings fluctuations due to their very nature. For example, the prospect of a change in the economic environment may have little effect on a firm's earnings this year, but the effect on long-run profit outlook may be profound. For purposes of this study, we will therefore treat the risk of an unanticipated change in profitability expectations as a second distinct source of investment risk which is separate from that which stems from strictly transitory earnings fluctuations. The relative significance of a change in long-run profit expectations warrants this separate consideration because a reassessment of long-run profitability will have a stock price effect of an order of magnitude ten times as great as that resulting from a similar but transitory departure of earnings from the level expected in a given period.

At this level of analysis the consideration of sources of risk is completed by listing, as the third source of uncertainty, the risk of unanticipated changes in the market equilibrium discount rates at which expected cash flows are implicitly capitalized in the capital market. Unanticipated changes in market equilibrium marginal rates of time preference, and similar changes in other equilibrium rates such as the market cost price of risk, and inflation, all combine to produce unanticipated changes in the capitalization rates at which future expected cash flows are discounted by the market. If we ignore, for the present, the problems presented in the finer points of capitalizing earnings which are expected in future periods in a world of stochastic capitalization rates, it is clear that unanticipated changes in capitalization rates cause unanticipated changes in market values of stocks and are therefore a source of risk for stock investors. Indeed, since changes in capitalization rates have long-term implications for valuation of future earnings, it is clear that this source of risk will vie with unanticipated changes in profit expectations in terms of relative importance in determining overall stock risk.

GROWTH AND RISK:
AN INTUITIVE INTRODUCTION

Having introduced a classification of sources of common stock investment risk which is suitable for purposes of later analysis, and having declared earlier that the objective of this book is to study the effect of corporate growth on common stock risk, it may be useful to complete the introduction of what follows by offering, at an intuitive level, the reasoning that leads to the theory that corporate growth is an important factor in determining investment risk. Consider, first of all, the effect of unanticipated changes in interest rates on the market values of bonds of various maturities. It is well known that the day-to-day, month-to-month, and year-to-year unanticipated changes in the market values of long-term bonds due to unanticipated changes in interest rate levels tend to be much greater for long-term bonds than for relatively short-term ones. The underlying cause of the increased price volatility of longer-term bonds is that the market value of a long-term bond depends largely on the present value of a cash flow promised in the relatively distant future as compared to a short-term bond. A given change in interest rates has an effect on the present value of a future cash flow, and the magnitude of the effect is a positive function of time that must expire before the promised payment is forth-coming. This observation is not a new one, having been first made by Macauley in 1938 when he proposed a statistic called "duration" to aid in comparing the interest rate elasticities of different bonds. More recent, however, is the notion that the same concept may be applied to compare the risks of investing in stocks of corporations with different expected growth rates. To the extent that the market value of common equity depends relatively more heavily on the present value of very remote earnings, or net cash flows, in the case of a rapidly growing firm, that market value will be more sensitive to a given change in the capitalization rates at which those remote earnings are discounted than in the case of a firm expected to grow more slowly. Thus, it is to be expected that firms committed to rapid growth policies will be more risky from the point of view of common stock investments than those following more conservative growth objectives, at least for that element of risk that stems from unanticipated changes in capitalization rates.

An even stronger case for a positive relationship between corpo-rate growth and stock risk due to stochastic capitalization rates becomes evident if we consider the basis for the market value of common stock in terms of the present value of income from existing corporate investments vs. the net present value of expected future corporate investment opportunities. The stock market value of the common equity of a firm for which investment opportunities are few is clearly based largely on the present value of income from existing investments. If the capitalization rate for the stock changes unexpectedly from 12 percent to 13 percent, for example, the present value of existing investments will fall by approximately 1/12th, or 8.5 percent, other factors being constant. Since the market value of the stock is made up mainly of the value of existing corporate investments, the value of the stock will fall a like amount. Now consider the opposite case, where the market value of a stock is made up almost entirely of the net present value of expected future investment opportunities where it is believed that equity can be raised through retention of earnings or new issues at a cost of 12 percent and invested to earn 14 percent on average. If an unexpected change in time preference, inflation rates, or the market price of risk, causes an unexpected change in the stock's capitalization rate from 12 percent to 13 percent, the net present value of expected future investments will decline by at least 50 percent, the amount by which the expected future quasi-rents have been reduced, in effect. It follows that the market value of the firm's stock will suffer a similar decline since it was based largely on the net present value of future investment opportunities. Again, the conclusion is that the investment in a rapidly growing firm's stock is a much riskier proposition than the investment in the firm that is not expected to grow as rapidly.

In addition to risk which stems from stochastic capitalization rates, corporate growth may have similar magnifying effects on risk which stems from unexpected changes in the market's assessment of long-run profitability. By way of analogy, think of a peculiar bond where the coupon rate is revised in a stochastic process at the end of each period. The risk of holding a stock is analogous to holding such a bond. The expected rate of return on corporate investments is updated during each period and corresponds to a stochastic change in coupon. Given an unchanging capitalization rate structure, the possible day-to-day or year-to-year gain or loss from holding a short-term bond of the type described would be less than that from holding a similar but long-term bond if both bonds undergo an unexpected change in the future coupon rate just before the end of the investor's holding period. Similar reasoning leads us to believe that the same may be true of stocks of rapidly growing firms relative to stocks of more slowly growing firms. A change in the expected profitability of a rapidly growing firm may be of greater relative importance to present value than a similar change in the expected profitability of a firm which is growing more slowly.

Finally, consideration of the proportional effect of changes in expected profitability on the present value of existing investment vs. the net present value of expected future investment reinforces the conclusions drawn above. For a growing firm, much of the market value of the common stock derives from the expectation of future investments that the firm will make with positive net present values. The more rapidly the firm is expected to undertake future investments, and therefore to grow, the greater will be the reliance on future positive net present value investments in the assessment of current market value, relative to a firm which is not expected to invest rapidly, and for which, therefore, the market value is based more heavily on the value of existing investments. If the expected return on existing equity investments of a firm falls from 14 percent to 13 percent, and the change is not transitory, the value of the existing investment will fall by approximately 1/14th, or 7.1 percent. The market value of common stock which is based on the present value of income from existing investment will fall by the same proportion. However, for a firm with rapid growth expected and whose stock has a market value based largely on the net present value of expected future investment opportunities, the consequence of a similar profitability change will be much more dramatic. If the original expected return on new equity investment is 14 percent, while the cost of equity capital to finance the investment is 12 percent, a 1 percent change in the long-run return outlook to 13 percent will cut the net present value of new investment by at least 50 percent. The rapidly growing firm's stock price, which is based largely on future positive net present value investment expectations will suffer a similar fate. Inevitably, the conclusion is again drawn that investment in a rapidly growing firm's stock is intuitively much riskier than investment in the stock of a firm with little or no expected growth.

The third source of investor risk, transitory differences between actual earnings and the level expected, is not believed to be greatly affected by the rate of corporate growth. Due to the current nature of any unexpected earnings outcomes, the effect is considered to be almost directly felt without any substantial magnification or moderation by corporate growth. A slightly negative growth-risk relationship may exist for this type of risk, simply because the market value of a rapidly growing firm is more heavily based on expected future positive net present value investments than on profits from existing investments. Therefore, any transitory departure of profits from expected levels is simply a smaller fraction of market value in the case of a more rapidly growing firm.

AN OVERVIEW OF THE STUDY

The preceding intuitive analysis is an attempt to outline for the reader the basis for more detailed inquiry into the issue of whether or not there is a causal relationship through which the degree of investment risk present in common stocks is affected by corporate growth. In the chapters that follow we attempt to narrow down the problem to one which is amenable to more explicit analysis. To start with, a step in that direction is made in Chapter II where we review traditional valuation theory for stocks with growing streams of expected dividends. Also reviewed there is the dividend policy controversy which stimulated its development. The chapter serves to narrow down the appropriate definition of growth to use in the study to one which reflects the rate of investment expected to be financed by retention of earnings plus new stock issues. In short, under the assumptions to be employed, which include the assumption that capital markets are perfectly competitive, there appears to be no reason to distinguish between the two sources of equity capital. Therefore, the growth rate appropriate to the study is the rate of growth of *total* earnings and dividends, which is independent of dividend policy, per se, rather than the growth of *per share* values, which is not. We consider that the dividend policy controversy may have inadvertently distracted theorists from a more general study of total corporate growth and its implications for risk and valuation theory.

In Chapter III we review other aspects of the dividend decision process, for completeness, and in order to obtain a basis on which to later model the dividend decisions which corporations make under conditions of fluctuating earnings.

Chapter IV begins the development of explicit analysis aimed at studying the effect of growth on stock risk. There we study the implications of corporate growth for investment risk which stems from changing capitalization rates. We show that the capitalization rate elasticity of holding period returns on common stocks is a positive function of corporate growth. In addition, we show that undiversifiable stock risk as measured by the market beta of single period capital asset pricing theory is also a positive function of the rate of corporate growth. We realize some of the problems which may be presented by using the single period capital asset pricing model in conjunction with multi-period valuation models. However, we feel the conclusions reached are sufficiently robust that they will continue to hold when subsequent analysis undertakes the much more difficult task of investigating the implications of corporate growth for stock risk in the context of a true multi-period general equilibrium model of capital asset prices.

Chapter V extends the analysis to include the treatment of risk of changing long-run profitability expectations and the risk due to transitory fluctuations in earnings. Stock risk due to changes in long-run profit expectations is found to be magnified by corporate growth. As predicted, growth has a small negative effect on risk which stems from transitory fluctuations in earnings.

Chapter VI through VIII are empirical in nature. Chapter VI reviews previous empirical research concerning the correlation between growth and stock risk. Chapters VII and VIII present empirical tests of our growth-risk hypothesis using Canadian and U.S. data, respectively.

Chapter IX presents a brief summary and conclusions.

Chapter II

A Review of Dividend Valuation Theory

I. INTRODUCTION

The purpose of this chapter is to review the previous work in theoretical dividend valuation models relevant to the present study. The review achieves three objectives. First, it serves as a background against which to develop and appraise our later theoretical and empirical models. Second, it clarifies the outstanding issues with respect to the effects of dividend and investment policy on the valuation of common stock. Third, the review facilitates the identification and articulation of problems in the extant theory where additional study may lead to important extensions to our knowledge.

The chapter contains five sections. Section II deals with stock valuation under complete certainty and is followed by Section III which discusses the introduction of uncertainty. Section IV attempts to deal with the literature on the dividend policy controversy. The last section summarizes the material in the chapter and the issues which remain outstanding in this controversial area of financial theory.

II. STOCK VALUATION UNDER CONDITIONS OF COMPLETE CERTAINTY

The economic foundation of valuation theory is the application of the theory of choice to the problem of allocating resources over time. The original work on this problem is due to Irving Fisher.[1] He assumed that the future is certain and discovered that if capital markets are perfect the general equilibrium interest rate that is applicable in each future period is equal to the marginal rate of time preference of each individual in that period. The theory is widely accepted as useful and it provides the economic rationale for discounting future income in order to arrive at its present value.

The application of Fisher's work to the problem of common stock valuation is presented in the classical work of Williams.[2] If the dividend per share of a stock at the end of period t is equal to D_t, and if i_t is the rate of interest that reflects the general equilibrium marginal rate of time preference of each individual during period t, then the value of the share at the end of period $t = 0$ is

$$P_0 = \lim_{n \to \infty} \left[\frac{D_1}{(1+i_1)} + \frac{D_2}{(1+i_1)(1+i_2)} + \dots + \frac{D_n}{\prod_{j=1}^{n}(1+i_j)} \right] \quad (2.1)$$

where $\prod$ indicates the product operator. Furthermore, if we assume that the dividend stream grows at a rate equal to g in every future period, expression (2.1) may be written

$$P_0 = \lim_{n \to \infty} \left[\frac{D_1}{1+i_1} + \frac{D_1(1+g)}{(1+i_1)(1+i_2)} + \dots + \frac{D_1(1+g)^{n-1}}{\prod_{j=1}^{n}(1+i_j)} \right] \quad (2.2)$$

and if the marginal rate of time preference is the same in every period

$$P_0 = \lim_{n \to \infty} \left[\frac{D_1}{1+i} + \frac{D_1(1+g)}{(1+i)^2} + \dots + \frac{D_1(1+g)^{n-1}}{(1+i)^n} \right]$$

$$= \lim_{n \to \infty} \frac{D_1}{i-g} \left[1 - \left(\frac{1+g}{1+i} \right)^n \right]$$

$$= \frac{D_1}{i-g}, i > g. \quad (2.3)$$

By invoking the assumptions of a constantly growing dividend stream and unchanging marginal time preference, the difficult problem of stock valuation has been reduced to a problem of more manageable complexity when the future is assumed to be certain. At this point, however, the question remains as to how the dividend growth rate is determined.

Dividend Growth From Earnings Retention

The extension of the foregoing valuation model to explicitly consider the contribution of earnings retention to dividend growth is due to Gordon and Shapiro.[3]

Let Y_1 denote the earnings per share in period 1 and let b denote the fraction retained by the firm for reinvestment at a rate of return equal to r. Then the earnings per share in period $t = 2$ are given by

$$Y_2 = Y_1(1 + br) \tag{2.4}$$

provided there is no new issue of stock.

The dividend per share in period 2 is therefore

$$\begin{aligned} D_2 &= Y_2(1 - b) \\ &= Y_1(1 - b)(1 + br) \\ &= D_1(1 + br) \end{aligned} \tag{2.5}$$

and we conclude that the dividend growth rate in period 2 is equal to br. If we assume that b and r apply to every period, equation (2.3) may be written

$$P_0 = \frac{D_1}{i - br}, i > br. \tag{2.6}$$

New Equity Financing

The extension of the growth valuation model to include continuous equity financing was provided independently by Miller and Modigliani,[4] and by Gordon.[5] The resulting models are identical except for notation. Since we have followed Gordon's notation above we will review his version with a slight modification which will prove convenient in later chapters.

Suppose a firm will retain a fraction b of earnings each period and, in addition, it will issue new stock equal to a fraction s of earnings each period. If *total* earnings in period 1 are X_1, the total earnings in period 2 are

$$X_2 = X_1(1 + br + sr) \qquad (2.7)$$

and the growth rate of total earnings is equal to $br + sr$. However, earnings and dividends *per share* grow at a slower rate since the number of shares increases with each new issue.

When a new issue is placed on the market with perfect knowledge of the future the price of the issue is equal to an amount which ensures that the new shareholders will receive a rate of return equal to i per period. However, the new investment earns a rate to return equal to r by assumption. In consequence, the previous shareholders experience an accretion to their equity which compensates them for relinquishing part of their rights to future quasi-rents of the firm.

Let v be the fraction of each new issue that accrues to previous shareholders. If X_2^1 denotes the *total* period 2 earnings to shares outstanding before the issue at the end of period 1 then

$$X_2^1 = X_1(1 + br + srv). \qquad (2.8)$$

Dividing by the number of shares we have the earnings per share,

$$Y_2 = Y_1(1 + br + srv). \qquad (2.9)$$

The corresponding dividend per share is

$$\begin{aligned} D_2 &= Y_2(1 - b) \\ &= Y_1(1 - b)(1 + br + srv) \\ &= D_1(1 + br + srv). \end{aligned} \qquad (2.10)$$

It follows that the dividend per share growth rate is now

$$g = br + srv. \qquad (2.11)$$

Gordon has shown that[6]

$$v = \frac{r - i}{r(1 - b - s)}, b + s < 1. \qquad (2.12)$$

Substituting (2.12) into (2.11) for v we have

$$g = \frac{(b+s)r(1-b) - si}{1-b-s}, b+s < 1, \qquad (2.13)$$

which is identical to equation (25) in Miller and Modigliani.[7] Furthermore, using (2.13) for g in (2.3) we obtain

$$P_0 = \frac{Y_1(1-b-s)}{i - br - sr}, i > br + sr, \qquad (2.14)$$

which is identical to (23) in Miller and Modigliani.[8]

III. INTRODUCTION OF UNCERTAINTY

The valuation model for growing dividend streams reviewed in Section II has the characteristic of being valid if the future is assumed to be known with perfect certainty. However, the most troubling aspect of estimating security values is the presence of a large amount of uncertainty with all of its implications. Therefore, unless uncertainty is adequately represented in an extension of the foregoing model even its usefulness as an abstract conceptual tool is questionable.

Certain-Equivalent Factors

Assume that investors are risk averse, have homogeneous beliefs with respect to the distribution of future dividend outcomes, and behave as if they are governed by the Von Neumann and Morgenstern expected utility maximizing hypothesis.[9] Then each stock is traded in perfectly competitive capital markets until a general equilibrium obtains where shares are valued as if each dividend expectation is replaced by its general equilibrium certain-equivalent amount and discounted by the general equilibrium marginal rate of time preference.[10] That is, the value of a share is given by

$$P_0 = \lim_{n \to \infty} \left[\frac{\alpha_1 E_0(D_1)}{1 + i_1} + \frac{\alpha_2 E_0(D_2)}{(1 + i_1)(1 + i_2)} + \cdots + \frac{\alpha_n E_0(D_n)}{\prod_{j=1}^{n}(1 + i_j)} \right] \qquad (2.15)$$

where

$E_0(D_t)$ = the current investor expectation of the dividend to be paid at the end of period t, and

α_t = the general equilibrium marginal rate at which the expected value, $E_0(D_t)$, can be exchanged for a certain payment at the end of t.

Assume that the marginal rate of time preference is unchanging over time and define *dividend specific* discount rates, k_t, such that the following identity holds for the particular stock in mind:[11]

$$\frac{1}{(1+k_t)^t} = \frac{\alpha_t}{(1+i)^t}, \text{ all t.} \tag{2.16}$$

Then we can write (2.15) as

$$P_0 = \lim_{n \to \infty} \left[\frac{E_0(D_1)}{1+k_1} + \frac{E_0(D_2)}{(1+k_2)^2} + \cdots + \frac{E_0(D_n)}{(1+k_n)^n} \right] \tag{2.17}$$

and a value, k, *exists* such that

$$P_0 = \lim_{n \to \infty} \left[\frac{E_0(D_1)}{1+k} + \frac{(E_0(D_2)}{(1+k)^2} + \cdots + \frac{E_0(D_n)}{(1+k)^n} \right]. \tag{2.18}$$

A further simplification is possible if we assume that the *dividend expectations* grow at the rate g per period. Then

$$P_0 = \lim_{n \to \infty} \left[\frac{E_0(D_1)}{(1+k)} + \frac{E_0(D_1)(1+g)}{(1+k)^2} + \cdots + \frac{E_0(D_1)(1+g)^{n-1}}{(1+k)^n} \right]$$

$$= \frac{E_0(D_1)}{k-g}, \quad k > g. \tag{2.19}$$

If we assume that the approximation

$$g = \frac{(b+s)r(1-b) - sk_t}{1-b-s} \tag{2.20}$$

holds where the values of b, s and r are expectations, then analogous to (2.14),

$$P_0 = \frac{E_0(Y_1)(1-b-s)}{k-br-sr}, \quad k > br + sr. \tag{2.21}$$

Equation (2.21) is the result of treating the stock valuation problem as one of determining the present value of a stream of dividend expectations which are assumed to grow at the rate g each period. As we will see in the next section, *if* k is independent of b, (2.21) may also be considered a total earnings valuation model. All that is required, in that case, is to multiply (2.21) by the number of shares outstanding to obtain the total value of the common stock as a function of total earnings less total investment in each period. This provides us with a preview of the very nature of the controversy over the relevance of dividend policy in valuation theory.

IV. THE EARNINGS VALUATION CONTROVERSY

In the preceding sections of this chapter we reviewed the development of a dividend valuation model which, we believe, has the twin attributes of being disarmingly simple and yet sufficiently well representative of the actual process of stock valuation to yield very robust insights. What we purposely ignored, however, is the heated controversy over whether dividend policy is irrelevant in stock valuation and therefore whether the valuation of earnings is actually equivalent to the valuation of dividends. Although the dividend valuation model is exceedingly well developed, if it can be shown that dividend policy is truly irrelevant, it may be that the process of stock valuation can be represented by an even simpler, and perhaps a more robust, earnings model. Therefore, a review of the controversy over the earnings valuation hypothesis is justified.

Prior to 1956, it is fair to say, the contribution of earnings retention to stock value was formally studied only in the theoretical context of a perfectly certain future and perfect capital markets. It is shown by Fisher's intertemporal investment and consumption model,[12] and well understood by others,[13] that earnings which are reinvested to earn the going rate of return on capital instead of being released for consumption neither add to nor subtract from the value of the overall stream of benefits. With the contemplation of the implications of uncertainty, however, the formerly solid case for ignoring dividend policy is somewhat weakened.

In 1954 Clendenin and Van Cleave[14] published a paper addressed to the problem of the valuation of growing dividend streams when the future is uncertain and they raised two points which have received a great deal of discussion. First, they noticed that if the future dividends of many companies were assumed to continue to grow at historical rates the value of their stocks were not finite when discounted at customary rates of return. Second, they hypothesized that greater than customary capitalization rates are applicable to the future dividends on "growth stocks" since "... many investors are skeptical and would probably wish to discount the very large and remote dividends in this perpetually growing series at a high discount rate."[15] That is, Clendenen and Van Cleave believed that investors would perceive remote dividends to be highly risky and therefore deserving of higher than usual discount rates. This theory implies that the previously accepted results of the Fisher model may not be robust in the absence of perfect prescience and that further supporting evidence based upon less restrictive assumptions is required if the earnings valuation hypothesis is to retain our acceptance in an uncertain world.

A further blow to the earnings hypothesis came in 1956 when Gordon and Shapiro[16] presented a simple model of the valuation of dividends with constant growth through reinvestment of retained earnings (our equation 2.21 with $s = 0$). This simple but powerful model accomplishes the following. First, it shows quite effectively the relationship between share value and the rate of return on reinvestment relative to the dividend capitalization rate in terms of the fraction of earnings retained. Second, it is strong support for the contention that at least some shares will have rapid dividend growth for a very long time since all that is required for such growth is a policy of earnings retention and the ability on the part of management to seek out attractive opportunities for reinvestment. Third, it shows that if capitalization rates are not a function of dividend growth rates then the probability of extremely high (if not infinite) share prices is surely much greater than the relative frequency with which such prices are actually observed.

As the explanation for this apparent contradiction between the indicated and observed frequency of very high share prices, Gordon and Shapiro hypothesized that average dividend capitalization rates are positively related to the rate of earnings retention. While the statement of a hypothesis doesn't necessarily mean it is so, and while there are other obvious reasons for a low relative frequency of extremely high stock prices (such as competitive entry and finite natural resources) the hypothesis appears reasonable enough to cause at least some doubt that the alternate earnings hypothesis is true.

In 1957 Durand[17] presented an analysis of the theoretical evidence against the earnings valuation hypothesis and concluded that capitalization rates are positively related to dividend growth for at least two reasons. It is interesting to note that one of the reasons he raised stands unchallenged in the literature since it was first presented.

First, Durand drew an analogy between the valuation of dividends which are large, but remote, elements of a growing dividend stream and the valuation of the income from a series of gambles as described in Bernoulli's "Exposition of a New Theory on the Measurement of Risk" first published in 1738.[18] He argued, in effect, that stocks with dividends that are expected to grow at a rate exceeding the customary capitalization rate have finite prices because of the principle of diminishing marginal utility of wealth. We now recognize that this is equivalent to adding a risk premium to the discount rate and for this reason remote dividends may be subject to higher capitalization rates than relatively current ones.

A second point made by Durand has its basis in previous work by Macauley.[19] Very briefly, Macauley observed that the holding period return of a bond has a component of risk which arises from changing interest rates and which varies with both its term to maturity and the size of its coupon payments. Therefore he proposed the statistic called duration with which to obtain a unique ranking of bonds that corresponds to their relative holding period risk. Duration is the weighted average term to maturity *of each payment* on a security where the weights are the present values of the payments. The statistic is an accurate indicator of the holding period risk of high-quality bonds provided the term structure of interest rates is assumed to always shift uniformly for all maturities.[20]

Durand's contribution in light of Macauley's work consists of an expression for the duration of a stream of constantly growing dividends and the conclusion that because stocks with rapidly growing dividends have very great duration their capitalization rates must be greater than those on securities of lesser duration.[21] In effect, Durand's point on duration is the following: Since the duration of a dividend stream is a positive function of its growth rate, the component of holding period risk that is due to changing capitalization rates increases with dividend growth in much the same way that the holding period risk of a bond increases with its term to maturity. This point is of major significance to the theory of stock valuation and we explore it much further in the chapters which follow.

The other side of the controversy over the effect of dividend policy, as we mentioned earlier, has its basis in the long-standing belief by many that the value of a firm is a function of its total earnings. This belief is well founded, as Fisher's model shows, provided the future is assumed to be perfectly certain and investment is either independent of retained earnings or retained earnings are reinvested at the rate of return required on capital. However, in 1959 Gordon[22] made a solid point concerning the earnings valuation hypothesis: Since dividends are the ultimate benefits that are received by the owners of a share of stock it is incontrovertible that "... the dividend [valuation] hypothesis is correct regardless of whether the earnings hypothesis is correct. The only point at issue is whether the dividend hypothesis is unnecessary. Can one study the pricing of common stocks and related questions without considering the fraction of income paid in dividends?"[23] He also makes the critical point that for the earnings valuation hypothesis to be correct the average capitalization rate for dividends must be independent of the earnings retention rate.

In 1961 Miller and Modigliani[24] presented a paper which is considered by many as a classic. It is widely accepted as proving the irrelevance of dividend policy by demonstrating the equivalence between approaches to share valuation based upon either future earnings, dividends, cash flows, or current earnings plus future investment opportunities. What is usually overlooked, however, is that their demonstration of the equivalence of these approaches assumes, by their own admission, that the future is perfectly certain. Furthermore, their attempt to extend their conclusions to a world where the future is uncertain fails in several crucial respects.

The first is a failure to admit *complete* uncertainty since there is no relaxation of their previous assumption to admit that general equilibrium capitalization rates are subject to change. Therefore they have not dealt with Durand's point that duration is a function of reinvestment policy and that what might be termed capitalization rate risk probably increases with duration.

Their second failure is that they fail to recognize *what* must be proven in order to support their earnings valuation hypothesis in a world of uncertainty. Gordon's point that they must prove that the dividend capitalization rate is independent of dividend policy is valid. If dividend policy does have an effect on the capitalization rate then the *capitalized value* of future dividends will change with a change in the dividend policy.

The third failure in the Miller and Modigliani proof under uncertainty is their failure to recognize the full implications of uncertainty for what investors can be assumed to believe regarding future earnings and dividend payout levels. It is perhaps reasonable to assume that investors believe future total earnings of two firms will be the same in every period. It is also reasonable to assume that investors expect dividends to be the same in every period if the current dividends of the two firms are equal. What is *not* reasonable is that investors will continue to expect the two firms will have identical future dividends in every period when the dividend payout of one firm is changed in the current period. To assume it is so is to implicitly assume that investors place no weight on current dividend payout rates in forming expectations about future payouts. Any conclusion from analysis based upon that assumption is so restricted that its usefulness in providing insights to stock valuation in the "real" world is seriously impaired.

The above three weaknesses in the Miller and Modigliani analysis raise doubts about the validity of their proof that dividend policy is irrelevant when the future is uncertain and investment is held constant. Nevertheless, their theorem may be true by the following reasoning: Equation (2.21) above is the Miller and Modigliani expression (23) on a per-share basis extended to include the assumption that earnings and dividends are uncertain and that it is the dividend per-share *expectations* that are assumed to grow at the constant rate given by (2.20).[25] That is

$$P_0 = \frac{E_0(Y_1)(1 - b - s)}{k - br - sr}, k > br + sr. \qquad (2.23)$$

In this model, the assumption that total investment is independent of dividend policy is operationalized by imposing the condition $db + ds = 0$.
Therefore

$$\frac{\partial P_0}{\partial b} = - \frac{E(Y_1)(1 - b - s)(\partial k / \partial b)}{(k - br - sr)^2} \qquad (2.24)$$

and share value is independent of the retention rate provided $\partial k / \partial b = 0$. Of course this last condition is what Gordon has always maintained must be proven for the earnings valuation hypothesis to be accepted as correct.[26]

Since the validity of the earnings hypothesis depends on whether or not the average discount rate is a function of the earnings retention rate when investment is held constant, we turn to the theoretical evidence on that question. First, recall that Durand has provided two arguments for the case that the risk adjusted discount rate for a future dividend expectation increases with its futurity. One has to do with the theory of diminishing marginal utility of wealth (risk aversion) and the theory that the uncertainty of future dividends increases with their futurity. The other argument by Durand is that changing capitalization rates cause capitalization risk and that capitalization risk increases with duration. It follows that the capitalization risk with respect to a future dividend expectation increases with its futurity. Therefore it seems reasonable to conclude that the risk adjusted capitalization rates applicable to dividend expectations may also increase with the futurity of the expectations. That is, where the value of a share is given by

$$P_0 = E_0(D_1) \sum_{t=1}^{\infty} \frac{(1+g)^{t-1}}{(1+k_t)^t} \tag{2.25}$$

it appears reasonable to conclude that $k_{t+1} > k_t$ for any t. If that is assumed to be true, it is clear that the average capitalization rate for a stream of dividend expectations is a positive function of its growth rate. Gangolli has offered a proof of it in an appendix to a paper by Gordon.[27] However, for the theorem to reject the earnings hypothesis, it must be proven under the assumption that investment is held constant, a fact which Gangolli overlooked. Moreover, what appears reasonable may not be true. In response to Robichek and Myers'[28] criticism of the use of risk adjusted discount rates, Chen[29] has shown that the capitalization rates applied to dividend expectations may *not* increase with their futurity. In order for $k_{t+1} > k_t$ to hold for any t in (2.25) not only is it necessary to show that risk increases with t, but also that risk increases *at an increasing rate*. Clearly this is a very difficult task and one which has not been accomplished to date.

While the contribution by Chen indicates that the behavior of capitalization rates for dividend expectations as a function of their futurity is not very clear, a more recent paper by Higgins[30] claims to show that the issue loses its significance when investment is held independent of dividend policy. Higgins offers a proof that the value of a firm is independent of dividend policy even if the capitalization rates for dividends are a function of their futurity. If the theorem is correct, the earnings valuation hypothesis cannot be rejected. However, his proof contains one of the same weaknesses which we earlier noted in the paper by Miller and Modigliani.

Specifically, Higgins' proof assumes that investors initially expect the future earnings and dividends for two firms will be identical. That assumption is reasonable and not restrictive in terms of the result. However, he also implicitly assumes that a change in the current dividend payout rate by one of the firms leaves the investors' expectations of future payout rates unchanged. As we noted in our review of the Miller and Modigliani paper, such an assumption brings the generality of the resulting theorem into serious question.

V. CONCLUDING REMARKS

The preceding sections of this chapter have briefly reviewed the evolution of a simple but very useful theory of stock valuation. The foundations of the model are contained in the classic contribution to capital theory by Irving Fisher with subsequent extensions by others to achieve more robust results with respect to common stocks under conditions of uncertainty.

A major part of the review is devoted to the controversy over whether valuation of stocks may be correctly viewed as simply a problem of determining the value of expected total earnings or whether the problem must be more properly considered as one of capitalizing expected dividends per share. The answer appears to be in establishing whether or not the average capitalization rate for dividends is a function of dividend policy when total investment is held independent of the amount of financing obtained from retained earnings.

From our review of the theoretical evidence presented by both sides to the controversy, we must conclude that neither case has been established. Proponents of the earnings valuation hypothesis have offered proof that their viewpoint is correct but we have noted serious weaknesses in their arguments. On the other hand, the case for asserting that dividend policy is in fact relevant has also not been conclusively established.

While the issue of the relevance of dividend policy, per se, is undoubtedly important, the absence of a final settlement of the question need not have such an overwhelmingly negative effect on the pursuit of further extensions to the theory of stock value as it seems to have had in the past. Indeed, it is perhaps possible to conclude that the issue has diverted theoretical attention away from the pursuit of research that will presently be seen to have much greater significance for stock valuation than the question of whether the earnings hypotheses is correct or not.

For instance, the intense concentration on the requirement that total investment be assumed exogenous to dividend policy has tended to draw attention away from the fact that the *rate of investment* is really endogenous to corporate policy. Lintner, for one, has recognized the endogenous nature of investment and he has obtained an interesting result which seems quite general.[31] He has shown that the optimal target rate of corporate growth is a function of the dispersion of future short period growth distributions and that the degree of serial correlation in short period growth rates is also an important determinant of optimal growth policy. This work shows that questions concerning corporate growth as an endogenous policy variable are important in terms of determining the risk of common stock. Our contribution in the analysis which follows is the development of a model for studying this question which takes advantage of the previous work which we have reviewed in this chapter in conjunction with widely accepted results in the modern theory of capital markets.

Chapter III

The Dividend Decision

I. INTRODUCTION

In the preceding chapter we concluded that financial economists have been unable to reach a concensus on whether or not dividend policy, per se, has an effect on stock valuation. However, it does seem to be widely accepted that firms pay dividends out of available earnings or cash flow according to relatively stable, long-run policies concerning the fraction of income to be distributed on average. There have recently been several studies of the dividend decision in which models of this process have been proposed and subjected to estimation and empirical tests. In this chapter we briefly review the state of knowledge concerning the dividend decision by reviewing the most important theoretical dividend policy models and some of the empirical results. The main objective of this review is to satisfy a need to understand and model the dividend decision in the analytical work which is presented in Chapters IV and V.

By way of an overview, we first present alternative models of the dividend decision in Section II. In Section III we review some of the empirical work aimed at estimating and testing the models.

In Section IV an extension to the theory is offered that improves the representation of the dividend process when a firm's earnings are growing at a steady rate. Section V is a review of the tests for information content in payout decisions and Section VI provides a summary and conclusions.

II. MODELS OF DIVIDEND PAYOUT

Partial Adjustment Model

The first formal model of the dividend decision attributes the observed smoothing of dividend payout by firms experiencing fluctuating earnings to a recognition by managers that fluctuating dividends are a source of dissatisfaction for stockholders.[1] Consequently, the payout of a fraction q of earnings is viewed as a target to be approached asymptotically when earnings fluctuate from period to period. If Y_t denotes earnings per share in period t, the target dividend payment is

$$D_t^* = qY_t. \tag{3.1}$$

However, the actual dividend to be paid is determined according to a partial adjustment process whereby the difference between D_t^* and the previous dividend is only partially eliminated. That is,

$$D_t - D_{t-1} = \gamma(D_t^* - D_{t-1}) + e_t, \tag{3.2}$$

where γ is a partial adjustment factor and e_t is a stochastic error term with zero expectation and no serial correlation.[2] Substituting (3.1) into (3.2) and rearranging, the period t dividend is stated in terms of period t earnings, the previous dividend, and the error term,

$$D_t = \gamma qY_t + (1 - \gamma)D_{t-1} + e_t, \tag{3.3}$$

or, in difference form,

$$\Delta D_t = D_t - D_{t-1} = \gamma qY_t - \gamma D_{t-1} + e_t. \tag{3.3a}$$

Adaptive Expectations Model

An alternative to the partial adjustment model of dividend payout proposed by Lintner is a model which attributes dividend smoothing to uncertainty and the discounting of unexpected changes in earnings by managers.[3] The model is somewhat analogous to Friedman's[4] permanent income hypothesis in that managers are thought to adopt a policy of distributing a fraction q of expected normal (permanent) earnings, the estimation of which is updated each period by giving some weight to the observed difference between current earnings and the previous expectation. If Y_t^* denotes expected normal earnings for period t, the dividend decision is

$$D_t = qY_t^* + v_t \tag{3.4}$$

where v_t is a stochastic error term with zero mean and no serial correlation. The adaptive expectations model for normal earnings is

$$Y_t^* - Y_{t-1}^* = \rho(Y_t - Y_{t-1}^*) \tag{3.5}$$

where ρ is the coefficient of adaptation. Substituting (3.4) for Y_t^* and Y_{t-1}^*, and rearranging, the partial adaptation model for dividends is

$$D_t = \rho qY_t + (1-\rho)D_{t-1} + v_t - (1-\rho)v_{t-1}. \tag{3.6}$$

The similarity between the reduced form of the partial adjustment model (3.3) and equation (3.6) is readily apparent. Although the theoretical grounds yielding the structural equations for the two models are quite dissimilar, the reduced form equations are identical except for the error terms. If the structural specification of the partial adjustment model is correct, the error term in (3.3) will be serially independent while, if the structural specification of the adaptive expectations model is correct, v_t will be serially independent causing the error term in (3.6) to have first order serial correlation.

Combined Partial Adjustment and Adaptive Expectations

It has been pointed out in a recent study by Roger Waud[5] that the partial adjustment model and the adaptive expectations model are not mutually exclusive. It is possible that dividends are paid according to both structural concepts and, if so, the result is a change in the reduced form equation.

Let the target dividend of the partial adjustment model be determined by normal earnings instead of actual earnings. That is,

$$D_t^* = qY_t^*. \tag{3.7}$$

Substituting this into (3.2) of the partial adjustment model yields the reduced form equation

$$D_t = \gamma qY_t^* + (1 - \gamma)D_{t-1} + e_t. \tag{3.8}$$

Substituting for Y_t^* from equation (3.5) of the adaptive expectations model

$$D_t = \gamma q[\rho Y_t + (1 - \rho)Y_{t-1}^*] + (1 - \gamma)D_{t-1} + e_t. \tag{3.9}$$

Now, lagging (3.8) one period, solving for Y_{t-1}^*, substituting the result into (3.9), and rearranging, we have the reduced form of the combined partial adjustment and adaptive expectations model,

$$\begin{aligned} D_t = \gamma\rho qY_t + [(1 - \rho) + (1 - \gamma)]D_{t-1} - (1 - \rho)(1 - \gamma)D_{t-2} \\ + [e_t - (1 - \rho)e_{t-1}]. \end{aligned} \tag{3.10}$$

Substituting recursively for lagged values of D_t, equation (3.10) may be transformed into a distributed lag on past earnings,

$$D_t = \gamma\rho q \sum_{j=0}^{\infty} \sum_{i=0}^{j} (1 - \rho)^{j-i}(1 - \gamma)^i Y_{t-j} + u_t, \tag{3.11}$$

where u_t is a composite error term.

From (3.10) and (3.11) it is apparent that ρ and γ enter the reduced form and the distributed lag function symmetrically. Therefore, it is impossible to distinguish between the two structural forms in empirical work. At best, it may be possible to estimate the product $\gamma\rho$ and the sum $\gamma + \rho$. Additional complications of this model for empirical research are examined by Waud in a simulation study.

Simulation of Dividend Policy Estimation with Specification Error

From the review of Waud's combined model it is clear that empirical estimation of either the partial adjustment model or the adaptive expectations model alone may be doomed to failure before it is undertaken. If both partial adjustment and adaptive expectation behavior is present in the formulation of dividend policy, it is not only impossible to distinguish between γ and ρ in (3.10), but, as has often been the case, if (3.3) or (3.6) is estimated, the result *may* be biased coefficient estimates due to specification error. This problem exists in addition to the problem of small sample bias that exists when one of the regressors is the lagged dependent variable (D_{t-1}). If the further problem of serially correlated errors is present, (3.6), this bias in small sample estimates extends to large samples as well.

In order to determine the magnitude of the bias when (3.10) is the true model and either (3.3) or (3.6) is estimated, Waud has simulated estimation of (3.3) with dividend data generated from (3.10) using an independently distributed error term with mean zero and unit variance. The Y_t were assumed stochastic and generated with mean zero and variance five. The dividend data were generated for ρ equal to 1.00, 0.80, 0.60 and 0.40. For *each* value of ρ, Waud generated 50 "time series" samples of 20 "periods," 30 "periods" and 60 "periods" for *each* value of γ equal to 0.25, 0.50 and 0.75. The target payout ratio was assumed equal to 1.0.

After thus generating the data to simulate dividend policy according to (3.10), Waud estimated the reduced form of the partial adjustment model (3.3). What he found is predictable from econometric theory. Where the data was generated with ρ equal to 1.00 the reduced form of the partial adjustment model produced very good estimates of γ with little, if any, bias for all three values of γ simulated by the data. For ρ equal to 0.6 the estimates were about 0.41 for true values of γ equal to 0.75, and 0.11 for true values of 0.25. The lower the value of ρ the poorer the estimate. The bias also tended to increase proportionately for smaller values of γ. Somewhat surprisingly, the results were independent of sample size.

The conclusion is that an estimate of γ using (3.3) yields estimates which are biased toward zero when ρ is less than one. The smaller the value of ρ the greater the bias and, at the same time, the smaller the true value of γ the greater the bias toward zero in proportional units. The same conclusion will hold if (3.6) is used to estimate ρ when γ is less than one. Econometric theory also indicates that the problem may be further compounded when the error term in (3.10) is serially correlated which is to be expected for most data.

Waud's simulation also provides information on the extent of potential bias in the estimate of q obtained using reduced forms such as (3.3) or (3.6). When ρ is equal to 1.00 in the simulated data generated by (3.10), the estimate of q is excellent for every value of γ. However, for data with ρ and γ both less than one, the estimate of q is biased upward reaching a maximum of 207% of its true value for ρ equal to 0.40 and for γ equal to 0.25. For ρ greater than 0.40 the results appear independent of sample size, but for ρ equal to 0.40 the greatest bias occurs for "short time series" samples. Again, the conclusion is that estimates of the target payout ratio, q, are potentially upward biased if reduced forms (3.3) or (3.6) are used under conditions which call for (3.10) as the correct empirical specification.

III. EMPIRICAL ESTIMATES

Prior to Waud's research which points to potential specification error in estimation of partial adjustment or adaptive expectations models, papers by Lintner, Darling and Brittain reported empirical research attempting to estimate (3.3) and variants thereon.[6] The work was mainly done with aggregate data, although Brittain reports estimates using individual firm data which did not refute his aggregate results. Later studies reported by Fama and Babiak, and Chateau, among others, used individual firm data and more sophisticated estimation techniques.[7]

Lintner

In the same paper where he proposed the partial adjustment dividend model, Lintner[8] reported briefly on empirical estimates of the coefficients using aggregate annual U.S. data as reported in the National Accounts for the period 1918–1941, omitting 1936–1937 due to the incidence of a special undistributed profits tax in those years. The coefficient estimates where profits were adjusted for inventory profits are

$$D_t = \$352.3 \times 10^6 + .15Y_t + .70D_{t-1} + u_t.$$

This regression estimate of (3.3) indicates $(1 - \gamma) = 0.70$ or $\hat{\gamma} = 0.30$ and $\hat{q} = .15/\hat{\gamma} = 0.50$. Attempts to add plant and equipment expenditures, change in current profits, and the greatest previous dividend when greater than D_{t-1} resulted in no additional explanatory power.

Darling

One year later Darling[9] reported on an attempt to further explain dividend policy by including depreciation and changes in sales over two previous years. The estimate with greatest explanatory power for aggregate annual data for 1921–1954 excluding 1936–1938 is

$$D_t = \$288 \times 10^6 + .148Y_t + .619D_{t-1}$$
$$(.018) \quad (.078)$$
$$+ .050A_t - .0047\Delta S_t, R^2 = .989.$$
$$(.055) \quad (.0017)$$

The coefficient estimates are similar in magnitude to those reported by Lintner. Depreciation failed to enter with a significantly positive coefficient but the change in sales over the previous two years enters with a significantly negative sign. This may be interpreted in light of modern investment theory as a proxy for desired change in capital stock to support increased output levels. However, changes in sales may also proxy for inflation which tends to make equipment replacement cost high relative to allowed depreciation. An examination of residuals convinced Darling that they were consistent with business expectations of future liquidity needs as described in business annuals of the period.

Brittain[10]

Brittain's excellent study of aggregate dividend payout rates for all corporations and for the manufacturing industry during

1942–1960 was primarily aimed at investigating the effect of changing depreciation policies on dividend policies. In the study, however, he also examined the effect of changes in corporate taxation, personal taxation, interest rates, sales, corporate liquidity and expenditures on plant and equipment.

Examination of trends in after-tax earnings, after-tax cash flow, and dividends for 1942–1960 shows that while profits calculated using tax return depreciation rates grew by 2% per year, aggregate dividends increased at an average annual rate of 5.8%[11] Brittain therefore hypothesized that cash flow, which grew at an average rate of 6 percent per year, would explain corporate dividend behavior much better than after-tax earnings. When the reduced form of the partial adjustment model (3.3a) was fitted to the data for all corporations in aggregate using official net profits (Y_t) in one version and cash flow (C_t) in another the results were,[12]

$$\Delta D_t = -\$583 \times 10^6 + .132\,Y_t - .147\,D_{t-1}, \bar{R}^2 = .61, \text{D.W.} = 1.79,$$
$$(293 \times 10^6) \quad (.027) \quad (.045)$$

and

$$\Delta D_t = 285 \times 10^6 + .158\,C_t - .540\,D_{t-1}, \bar{R}^2 = .80, \text{D.W.} = 1.90.$$
$$(168 \times 10^6) \quad (.020) \quad (.074)$$

A much larger estimate is obtained for γ in the cash flow version (0.540) than for the official profits case (0.147). The $\bar{R}^2$ is much higher for the cash flow version and the Durbin-Watson statistic shows less serial correlation for the latter model as well. However, the advantage in using cash flow shows up most dramatically when the estimated target payout ratios are calculated. For the profits version, the estimate for q is $.132/.147 = 0.90$, which is very high compared with the ratio of total dividends to total profits for the period which is 0.50. The profit version estimate of q seems to be about 80 percent higher than the actual payout ratio. For the cash flow version, the estimate of q is $.158/.540 - 0.29$, which is very close to the actual fraction of cash flow paid out (0.30).

In summary, Brittain has shown that cash flows perform much better than official profits computed from taxation return depreciation rates, in explaining aggregate corporate dividend payout during the period 1942–1960. Virtually identical results were also reported for the manufacturing sector. The conclusion to be drawn, at least for the period studied which was one of great changes in depreciation policies, is that a cash flow version of the partial adjustment model explains aggregate dividend payout quite well. Moreover, a comparison of the estimate of the target payout rate with the actual fraction of cash flow paid out leads to the conclusion that there is little, if any, bias in the cash flow estimates which Waud's[13] study warned against. Therefore, although it is impossible to distinguish between the partial adjustment model and the adaptive expectations model on an empirical basis, the Brittain results offer support for the theory that only one of these models is required as opposed to the case of a combination as hypothesized by Waud. The evidence supporting this conclusion is the apparent absence of any upward bias in the estimate of the aggregate target payout ratio using the cash flow version of income.

In further empirical work aimed at exploring other determinants of dividend policy Brittain found that the dividend payout ratio is a negative function of personal income tax rates, interest rates and two-year rates of change in sales. No effect was found for expenditures on plant and equipment or changes in corporate liquidity. The negative effect of interest rates may indicate increased retention of earnings during periods of tight money or, since interest rates are closely correlated with inflation, the effect may be a reflection of the inadequacy of depreciation as an allowance for the cost of replacing plant and equipment at inflated prices. The negative effect on dividends of increasing sales is the same as that reported earlier by Darling[14] and may be due to forecasted need for increased investment in assets to support higher sales. It may also be a proxy for inflation since sales are a function of price levels. Finally, the negative effect of increased personal income tax rates is explained by the widely accepted theory that retained earnings capital has a lower cost relative to other sources of capital when capital gains are taxed at lower rates than dividends.

Fama and Babiak

Although Brittain reported studies for industry and individual firm aggregation levels which gave some support to his study of aggregate data, the first comprehensive empirical study at the individual firm level is by Fama and Babiak.[15]

A preliminary examination of the relative frequency of dividend per share increases and decreases conditional on 6,246 observations of current and lagged profit changes provides evidence to support the notion of the lagged relationship between dividends and earnings which is implicit in both the partial adjustment model and the adaptive expectations model. However, examination of the relative frequency of increases and decreases in earnings per share conditional on previous changes supports the hypothesis that changes in annual earnings of individual firms are "nearly independent."[16] If that is true, and it does seem so from the evidence, structural equation (3.5) of the adaptive expectations model,

$$Y_t^* - Y_{t-1}^* = \rho(Y_t - Y_{t-1}^*), \qquad (3.5)$$

can be written as

$$Y_t^* = Y_t \qquad (3.5a)$$

since $\rho = 1.0$. That is, *the adaptive expectations model is part of dividend policy formulation*[17] *in combination with partial adjustment, but expectations are fully adaptive to the most recently observed value.* Since $\rho = 1.0$ is supported by the evidence, Waud's combination model reduces to that of partial adjustment in reduced form and the estimation bias against which he warns should not be of concern. This seems to be upheld by the apparent absence of upward bias in the target payout ratios estimated by Brittain using aggregate cash flow income which we discussed earlier. The result has important implications for our analysis of the effect of corporate growth on stock risk which is presented in Chapter V. It is also important for Fama and Babiak's study since it allows their estimation to proceed without presenting the near multi-collinearity problems associated with entering a second lagged dividend variable as in (3.10) when one lagged dividend is already present.

Accordingly, Fama and Babiak fitted reduced form (3:3a) to 19 years of annual data for each of 392 firms. The average value for R^2 is 0.432, the average estimate for γ, the partial adjustment coefficient, is .366 and the average target payout estimate was

0.46. Here again there is little evidence of an upward bias, indicating support for the partial adjustment model combined with a *fully* adaptive expectations model.

Contrary to Brittain's result using aggregate data, an attempt to fit (3.3a) using cash flow instead of net income resulted in reduced R^2 values, on average. Moreover, introduction of depreciation as an additional variable to net income failed to produce significantly positive coefficients on average. Indeed, at least 25 percent of the depreciation coefficient estimates had the incorrect sign. When the usually insignificant constant in the regressions was suppressed the R^2's were reduced materially on average, although the conditional out-of-sample prediction power of the regressions increased slightly.

According to Waud's[18] model combining partial adjustment and adaptive expectations, if ρ in (3.10) is less than 1.0 (less than *fully* adaptive expectations), the appropriate regression includes dividends lagged twice as well as once. Fama and Babiak fitted the empirical counterpart to (3.10) alternately using dividends lagged twice, earnings lagged twice and both lagged twice. On average the additional variable(s) took on coefficients with the incorrect sign and they were seldom significantly different from zero. Although these regressions suffered from near multicollinearity, the results are further support for the theory that earnings expectations are *fully* adaptive to latest observed values.

Finally, Fama and Babiak generated data using autocorrelated error terms and a growth trend since the data showed that the earnings grew on average during the period studied. Regressions fitted to the simulated data showed that estimation with a lagged dependent variable and a small amount of serial correlation in error terms did not produce serious bias. However, an attempt to estimate the growth trend in the simulated data through regression coefficient estimates was very inefficient.

In summary, the Fama and Babiak results lead to the conclusion that a fully adaptive expectations model for earnings together with a partial adjustment model for dividends is close to the truth. They have shown that the partial adjustment model using net income fits corporate data well on average and that the small amount of serial correlation in residuals presents no serious problem in estimating dividend policy parameters. Although estimation error appears quite high for individual firms as opposed to aggregate data, on average the estimates appear relatively unbiased and yield similar results for average partial adjustment factors and target payout rates to those obtained from regressions using aggregate dividend and profit data.

Chateau

Jean-Pierre Chateau has recently completed empirical studies of dividend payout policies that are similar in many respects to the study by Fama and Babiak. However, Chateau has used Canadian data and has been more concerned with the econometric techniques appropriate for producing unbiased parameter estimates in regressions with a lagged dependent variable and serially correlated error terms.

Using cash flow and dividend data for 40 firms for the period 1947 to 1970, Chateau estimated reduced form (3.10) to test for Waud's combined partial adjustment-adaptive expectations model. Only three of 40 firms gave a significant coefficient on D_{t-2}, indicating that the problem was not serious. Moreover, when D_{t-2} was omitted as in reduced form (3.3), the coefficient estimates were not substantially changed after correction for serially correlated error terms with the Hildreth-Lu procedure.[19] This result supports the theory of fully adaptive profit expectations discussed above in our review of the Fama and Babiak results.

In order to obtain efficient and unbiased estimates of corporate policy formulation parameters, Chateau used, among others, a procedure suggested by Feldstein called Augmented Least Squares.[20] The procedure consists of three steps.[21] First, for each firm, the instrumental regression

$$D_t = \alpha_0 + \alpha_1 C_t + \alpha_2 C_{t-1} + e_t \qquad (3.12)$$

is estimated to obtain "error free" estimates,

$$\hat{D}_t = D_t - \hat{e}_t. \qquad (3.13)$$

Next, the second stage regression

$$D_t = \beta_0 + \beta_1 C_1 + \beta_2 \hat{D}_{t-1} + u_t \qquad (3.14)$$

is estimated to obtain estimates of the residuals, $\hat{u}_t$, obtained from the consistent two stage regression procedure. Lastly, the augmented regression

$$D_t = \beta_0 + \beta_1 C_1 + \beta_2 D_{t-1} + \sum_{j=1}^{n} \rho_j \hat{u}_{t-j} + \varepsilon_t \qquad (3.15)$$

is run where j is selected to maximize the adjusted coefficient of determination. The effect of including the $\hat{u}_{t-j}$ variables in (3.15) is to overcome the specification problem which leads to serially correlated residuals in ordinary least squares. The estimates of (3.15) are consistent (unbiased in large samples) and more efficient than those obtained by the two stage procedure which terminates with (3.14).

The results of (3.15) as reported by Cheateau for 40 firms show an average value for the speed of adjustment coefficient, γ, equal to 0.379 and a target payout ratio, q, equal to 0.316. The actual average payout rate for the firms over the period of the study was 0.275 indicating the possibility of an upward bias in the estimates of q due to misspecification, either due to less than fully adaptive earnings expectations, as cautioned by Waud, or another error, such as incorrect treatment of earnings growth expectations, which we discuss in the following section.

IV. PARTIAL ADJUSTMENT OF DIVIDENDS WITH GROWTH EXPECTED

In his studies of the partial adjustment dividend model, Chateau[22] introduces the concept of constant growth expectation and reintroduces a dynamic growth model that is originally due to Kuh.[23] Rewriting (3.3) as

$$D_t = (1 - \gamma)^t D_0 + \gamma q \sum_{T=1}^{t} (1 - \gamma)^{t-T} Y_T \qquad (3.16)$$

and assuming that income has grown at a constant rate, g, so that

$$Y_t = Y_0(1 + g)^t, \tag{3.17}$$

the dividend at the end of period t may be written as

$$D_t = [D_0 - \gamma q Y_0(1 + g)/(\gamma + g)](1 - \gamma)^t + \frac{\gamma q Y_t(1 + g)}{\gamma + g}. \tag{3.18}$$

With a long history of steady growth the first term of (3.18) is very small with the result that the average actual payout ratio may be compared with the target payout ratio according to this model,

$$\frac{D_t/Y_t}{q} = \frac{\gamma(1 + g)}{\gamma + g}. \tag{3.19}$$

Thus $D_t/Y_t < q$ for $g > 0$ and $\gamma < 1$.

The above result seems to indicate that the fraction of earnings paid out in the form of dividends will always be less than the target payout ratio when growth is taking place and the partial adjustment coefficient is less than 1.0. At first thought, this result may seem reasonable since firms with growth objectives may be expected to retain a greater fraction of earnings than firms without opportunities for growth. However *that* is not the reason behind the result obtained by Kuh[24] and reproduced by Chateau,[25] which is due, instead, to a basic fault in applying (3.3) to a growth situation in the first place.

In assuming that (3.3) can be applied to a situation of expected growth in earnings, the assumption is implicit that (3.2) is an adequate model of the adjustment process when dividends are expected to grow. That is, dividends are assumed to adjust only partly to an *unexpected* change in the level of the target dividend brought about by a departure of earnings from the expected level, *and* also partly to an *expected* change in the level of the target dividend due to the growth trend. It is the assumed partial adjustment to *expected* growth that leads to the result presented by Kuh and Chateau.

An improvement to the partial adjustment model to correctly incorporate growth expectations is an assumption that dividends adjust fully to expected growth in dividends and only partly to unexpected departures in earnings from the expected growth trend. Such a partial adjustment model to replace (3.2) in a growth situation is

$$D_t - (1 + g)D_{t-1} = \gamma[D_t^* - (1 + g)D_{t-1}] + e_t. \qquad (3.20)$$

Substituting for D_t^* from (3.1), and rearranging, the reduced form equation is

$$D_t = \gamma q Y_t + (1 - \gamma)(1 + g)D_{t-1} + e_t, \qquad (3.21)$$

or, in difference form,

$$\Delta D_t = \gamma q Y_t + (g - \gamma g - \gamma)D_{t-1} + e_t. \qquad (3.21a)$$

It is clear from (3.21) and (3.21a) that any attempt to estimate (3.3) or (3.3a) for firms with growth expectations will result in an estimate of γ which is biased toward zero and an estimate for q which is biased upward. For example, on the basis of sample average estimates in the Chateau study, if $\hat{\gamma}$ equals 0.38 on the basis of estimating (3.3), and if the average growth rate is 6 percent, an estimate on the basis of (3.21) would yield $(1 - \gamma)(1.06) = 0.62$ or $\hat{\gamma} = 0.42$. The improved estimate of q would then be 0.28 as opposed to 0.31.

V. INFORMATION CONTENT OF DIVIDENDS

When Lintner[26] introduced the seminal concept of partial adjustment in dividend policy formation, he indicated that, while management regarded current earnings as the major factor in the dividend decision, another factor was the perceived ability of the firm to avoid cutting the dividend rate in the future. The assessment of this ability to sustain the payout rate is achieved through forecasts of sales growth and other factors which affect corporate liquidity. Thus, Lintner was suggesting that dividend decisions might be based on special information not available in current or past earnings data. Thus, dividend announcements may contain information that is not otherwise available to the public. Moreover, in the interest of understanding dividend policy formation, the question of whether managers take account of future profitability in dividend decisions is interesting in itself, as well as being of some importance in empirical tests of valuation models.

The first clear statement of the hypothesis that dividends may contain information on earnings potential that is not available in announced earnings is by Modigliani and Miller. In a later paper it was more fully discussed by the same authors and even later the concept was used but not tested in their empirical study of the cost of capital to electric utilities.[27] However, it was not until the early 1970's that the information content of dividends was rigorously tested. The following is a brief review of some of this work.

Pettit

Tests aimed explicitly at discovering the information effect of dividends have taken two forms. One method is to attempt to determine whether the announcement of dividend changes has an effect on the holding period return on the stock after adjusting for the movement in the market. The second is an attempt to discover whether unexpected dividend changes are capable of predicting future earnings more successfully than predictions using current and past earnings. Two studies have employed the method of standardized holding period returns and at least two have used a forecast of future earnings test.

Pettit[28] appears to be the first to examine the effects of dividend announcements, per se, although an earlier paper by Fama, Fisher, Jensen and Roll[29] studied the effects of dividend announcements which followed stock split announcements. In the interest of conserving space, we will simply report on some of the Pettit study results.

On a daily basis, Pettit adjusted the holding period returns on stocks for ten days on each side of a dividend announcement for 135 such announcements. The adjustment was to remove the effect of overall market movements and was done on the basis of each stock's return volatility relative to the market, as estimated from observations taken before and after the period under study for each stock. Then, by averaging the "abnormal" return performance relative to day − 10 for each of several ranges of dividend changes, the average specific effect due to the announcements was obtained. Thus, from the close of day − 1 to the close of day + 1 relative to the announcement day, for 22 firms with an announced dividend change of − 1 percent to − 99 percent the investors holding the stocks suffered an average loss of 6.20 percent. Surprisingly, 22 firms which announced an omitted dividend saw their stock fall an average of only 2.23 percent in the same length of time. The relatively small average loss in this case may be due to the tendency for such dramatic information to be "leaked" prior to the announcement. Other announcements had little effect, on average, with the largest effect for those stocks with an increase in dividend of 1 percent to 10 percent which resulted in an average positive abnormal return equal to 2.02 percent over the two days. In every case the major effect, if any, occurred on the announcement date or the following day with little advance effect and little subsequent effect. The conclusion is that the effect of dividend announcements on stock prices is only major for the case of an announced reduction in the dividend rate.

Pettit also studied the month by month abnormal performance of stocks with dividend change announcements. However, although he split the data into firms with earnings increases and earnings decreases, the effect of dividend announcements tends to be confounded with that from earnings information and it is difficult to draw a firm conclusion on the information content of dividends from the results presented. The following study attempted more care to abstract from earnings data effects.

Watts

Both abnormal returns and earnings forecast tests were conducted in a study of dividend information content by Watts.[30] In order to abstract from earnings effects, the unexpected annual dividend, given annual earnings, was estimated for each of 310 firms by running the following regression on annual data for the period 1945 to 1968,

$$\Delta D_t = \beta_1 D_{t-1} + \beta_2 Y_t + \beta_3 Y_{t-1} + e_t. \tag{3.22}$$

Then, after adjusting monthly holding period returns on each
stock for market movements according to relative volatility, the
average abnormal return was calculated relative to fiscal year end
for all annual dividend observations where the unexpected dividend
amount was positive and, likewise, for all where the residual of
(3.22) was negative. The outcome was no significant cumulative
abnormal return. Hence, the conclusion is that the hypothesis of
no information content in dividends could not be rejected by the
data employed. Watts concedes that a more conclusive test would
require daily dividend and price data such as employed by Pettit.[31]

Earnings Forecasts Using Dividends

Watts[32] was also one who studied the potential for using dividends to forecast future earnings. If dividends contain information
on future profits that is not present in current and past earnings,
dividends should forecast earnings better than past earnings.

Watts estimated the following regression for each firm in the
sample,

$$\Delta Y_{t+1} = \alpha_0 + \alpha_1 e_t + v_t, \qquad (3.23)$$

where e_t is the residual from the regression denoted in (3.22).
The average value of $\hat{\alpha}_1$ was 0.508 and the average t statistic was
0.406 with 10 percent of the regressions having a significantly
positive coefficient. Thus, any indication of information in dividends that is not also in earnings is weak. Others have produced
similar weak results.[33]

Watts concludes his paper by studying the reasons why a strong
informational content cannot be confirmed. He concludes that
by only partly adjusting dividends to reflect changes in profitability,
the extent of any dividend change that could be due to correct
managerial information is small and difficult to discern amid the
random unexpected changes that occur for numerous other
reasons. This is probably true, especially since special information
of any real significance may also be relatively rare.

One additional reason that attempts to forecast earnings changes
using dividend information must fail is due to the nature of the test.
Since the payment of a large dividend per share results in a reduced

amount of retained earnings, the subsequent earnings will be reduced through the use of additional alternate financing sources or due to foregone investment. Thus, any increase in profitability realized on a rate of return basis will be offset by a reduced per share equity capital stock when it comes to calculating the earnings per share. Consequently, the conclusion is well founded that the profitability forecasting ability of dividends has yet to be tested.

IV. SUMMARY AND CONCLUSION

In this chapter we have reviewed the literature concerned with modelling the corporate dividend decision as a dynamic process. The models we reviewed were inspired, for the most part, by the seminal work of John Lintner[34] who proposed the partial dividend adjustment model on the basis of a wideranging study of corporate characteristics which terminated with a set of personal interviews of corporate executives and a test of the model using aggregate data. The major competing model to the one proposed by Lintner is the adaptive expectations model in which managers are thought to pay out a constant fraction of normal (or permanent) earnings, estimates of which are updated according to an adaptive learning model when new earnings figures are observed. This model is somewhat analogous to the permanent income hypothesis of Milton Friedman.[35]

A potentially significant extension to the literature by Roger Waud[36] pointed out that the partial adjustment and adaptive expectations models are not mutually exclusive since dividend decisions may reflect both adaptive earnings expectations and partial adjustment of dividends to target levels each period. However, an empirical implication of the combination model does not appear to be consistent with the data, in that estimates of the reduced form of either the partial adjustment model or the adaptive expectations model do not appear to produce seriously biased coefficients as predicted. Additional evidence by Fama and Babiak[37] supports the hypothesis that earnings expectations are *fully* adaptive since they show that *changes* in the level of corporate earnings are very nearly serially independent. The conclusion is that Lintner's partial adjustment model is the correct version and that the target dividend is determined on the basis that latest earnings figures fully reflect normal earnings levels.

Additional factors, which appear to reduce the proportion of earnings paid out as dividends include the differential between personal taxation rates on dividends and capital gains, increases in corporate sales levels, and high interest rate levels. On the other hand, use of accelerated depreciation tends to increase dividends as a fraction of earnings.

In extensive econometric studies of the appropriate technique to employ in estimating the partial dividend adjustment model, both Feldstein and Chateau concluded that augmented least squares is the most efficient method of obtaining unbiased results. On the basis of a study of 40 Canadian firms, Chateau estimates an average payout target rate of 32 percent of cash flow. However, a correction of the model to incorporate a growth trend reduces this to about 28 percent, which corresponds to the average historical rate during the period of the study.

The notion that dividend decisions may reflect management information that is not available from earnings data is widely accepted on an intuitive basis. However, with the exception of announcements of dividend reduction, the presence of a useful information content has yet to be discovered. This failure on the part of researchers to find more evidence of an information content in dividend decisions may be due to problems with the empirical techniques employed, particularly where the tests are for a positive correlation between "unexpected" dividend changes and future earnings changes. It is probably fair to say that the earnings forecasting ability of dividend announcements has not been sufficiently well tested to rule out the theory that managers include their forecasts of future profitability in their dividend decision process. If this is the case, a model of dividend decisions should reflect a process whereby dividends are partially adjusted from previous levels to asymptotically approach the target payout rate for normal earning levels, based upon latest earnings figures and additional information which managers may regard as useful in forecasting future profitability.

Chapter IV

Growth and Capitalization Risk

I. INTRODUCTION

In this chapter we begin the development of a theory of the relationship between corporate growth and the risk incurred by an investor purchasing common stock. For purposes of presenting the theory we will adopt the premise that the risk of any common stock has three fundamental sources which can be separated conceptually although they are actually closely interrelated in real experience.

The first and certainly most familiar source of risk to common stockholders is the uncertainty associated with the level of earnings to be realized during the investor's holding period. This uncertainty may not only affect the cash flow to shareholders through the dividend, which we assume is always paid at the end of the holding period, but it may also affect the amount of earnings reinvested which form part of the basis for future earnings. This latter affect is transmitted to shareholders as part of the uncertainty associated with the closing share price that will be realized at the end of the holding period.

In addition to uncertainty concerning the earnings or return on net worth during the holding period there is always a good deal of risk concerning the closing price of the stock which stems from at least two other sources. One is the matter of expected return on net worth for the long-run future. At the beginning of the holding period part of investor risk stems from uncertainty about how the future prospects of the company will appear when the holding period is over. An unanticipated change in long-run profitability expectations can have a major effect on the holding period return through an effect on share price. Since it stems from changing profitability it may be convenient to refer to this risk as profitability risk while the first type of risk from uncertain holding period earnings might be called earnings risk.

The third conceptually separable type of risk of holding common stocks, and the one we will concentrate on in this chapter, will be called capitalization risk since it arises because of the propensity of capitalization rates for future dividends to undergo unanticipated changes. For example, when an investor purchases a share of stock at price P_{t-1} at the end of period $t - 1$ (start of period t) a great part of the risk he faces with respect to the holding period return, we believe, is the risk of a change in the market capitalization rate during the holding period. This leads to a considerable degree of uncertainty as to the value that will be placed in the stock at the end of the holding period and thus it affects the holding period return in a major way.

The history of the study of the effect of changing capitalization rates on common stock value is a varied one at best with few, if any, useful insights having been obtained until very recently. The whole problem behind the lack of success has been a failure to recognize all the implications of the complex process which generates expected dividend growth, although the process has been outlined in detail by Miller and Modigliani,[1] and by Gordon,[2] some time ago. A recent paper by Fewings[3] makes use of this basic material and sheds some light on the nature of the relationship between capitalization risk and corporate growth.

As we noted in Chapter II, there was a limited attempt to employ Macauley's duration concept to the study of the capitalization risk of holding common stocks. Durand[4] observed that Macauley[5] had proposed a present-value-weighted average period to maturity of all future cash receipts as a relative measure of the interest rate risk of investing in bonds having different maturities and coupon rates. Consequently, he proposed the same statistic to reflect the relative capitalization risk of investing in stocks with different dividend growth rates. The proposal was very close to the mark, but it missed for the following reason: For any security where the future payments are *independent of the capitalization rate*, Macauley's duration statistic is equal to the elasticity of the value of the security with respect to the capitalization factor.[6] If we define α_0 as the capitalization factor, the present value of a stream of n cash flows equal to C_t at the end of each period is given by

$$V_0 = \alpha_0 C_1 + \alpha_0^2 C_2 + \ldots + \alpha_0^n C_n. \quad (4.1)$$

If $C_1, C_2, \ldots, C_n$ are independent of α_0, the elasticity of V_0 with respect to α_0 is

$$\varepsilon(V_0, \alpha_0) = \frac{\partial V_0}{\partial \alpha_0} \cdot \frac{\alpha_0}{V_0} = [C_1 + 2\alpha_0 C_2 + \ldots + n\alpha_0^{n-1} C_n] \cdot \frac{\alpha_0}{V_0}$$

$$= \frac{\alpha_0 C_1 + 2\alpha_0^2 C_2 + \ldots + n\alpha_0^n C_n.}{V_0} \quad (4.2)$$

This is Macauley's present-value-weighted average period to maturity, or duration, although he proposed it from an intuitive argument without realizing its economic basis. As such it is a very useful measure of the relative interest rate risk of holding different bonds.[7] However, the elasticity of common stock value is not equal to the duration statistic because dividend expectations are not independent of the capitalization factor when the company is expected to issue new equity in the future. Consider a stock where expected dividends grow at a constant rate forever. Miller and Modigliani, and also Gordon, have shown that if earnings are certain the growth rate of dividends per share is given by[8]

$$g_0 = \frac{(b + s)r(1 - b) - sk_0}{1 - b - s} \quad (4.3)$$

Since by definition

$$\alpha_0 = \frac{1}{1 + k_0} \quad (4.4)$$

we have

$$\frac{dk_0}{d\alpha_0} = -\frac{1}{\alpha_0^2} \qquad (4.5)$$

and

$$\frac{\partial g_0}{\partial \alpha_0} = \frac{s}{(1 - b - s)\alpha_0^2}. \qquad (4.6)$$

The growth rate of expected dividends is a function of the capitalization factor and so (4.2) does not apply to common stocks. While the capitalization elasticity of common stock value may be a meaningful statistic we conclude that Macauley's duration statistic is not.[9]

Recognizing that the elasticity concept may provide additional insights for our study of the relationship between growth and stock risk, we proceed to study it from the viewpoint of the holding period return in Section II. This is a more complete approach and we find that corporate growth does contribute to capitalization risk, although it is not the growth rate of expected dividends per share that is important but rather the growth rate of *total* earnings and dividends generated by a company.

In Section III the concept of capitalization risk is examined in terms of the Capital Asset Pricing Model. An expression for holding period return is substituted into the expression for the covariance of the return on a stock with the return on the market portfolio of stocks. This covariance or systematic risk is also a positive function of the rate of growth of total earnings and dividends.

II. CAPITALIZATION FACTOR ELASTICITY OF HOLDING-PERIOD RETURNS

Assume for the present that unexpected changes in the capitalization rates for expected dividends are perfectly correlated for all common stocks and therefore the capitalization risk of a stock is completely undiversifiable. If that is true, the capitalization risk of a stock is directly related to the elasticity of its holding period return with respect to the capitalization factor at the end of the holding period. Our objective here is to examine that elasticity as a function of fundamental corporate variables related to the expectation of corporate growth. We assume that corporate leverage is constant as a fraction of common equity and that the rate of return on common equity is certain for all future periods.

By definition, the holding-period return relative on a stock is given by

$$R_t = \frac{1}{P_{t-1}}(D_t + P_t) \tag{4.7}$$

where the dividend is assumed to be paid at the end of period t. According to equation (2.19) the price of a share of stock at the end of period $t - 1$ is given by

$$P_{t-1} = \frac{E_{t-1}(D_t)}{k_{t-1} - g_{t-1}}, k_{t-1} > g_{t-1}. \tag{4.8}$$

Since period t earnings are certain once the common equity is established at the end of period $t - 1$, dividends are perfectly predictable one period in advance. Therefore,

$$E_{t-1}(D_t) = D_t \tag{4.9}$$

and

$$P_{t-1} = \frac{D_t}{k_{t-1} - g_{t-1}}, k_{t-1} > g_{t-1}. \tag{4.10}$$

Similarly

$$
\begin{aligned}
P_t &= \frac{D_{t+1}}{k_t - g_t} \\
&= \frac{D_t(1 + g_t)}{k_t - g_t}, k_t > g_t.
\end{aligned}
\tag{4.11}
$$

Substituting (4.10) and (4.11) into (4.7)

$$
\begin{aligned}
R_t &= \frac{(k_{t-1} - g_{t-1})}{D_t}\left[D_t + \frac{D_t(1 + g_t)}{k_t - g_t}\right] \\
&= \frac{(k_{t-1} - g_{t-1})(1 + k_t)}{k_t - g_t}, k_{t-1} > g_{t-1}, k_t > g_t.
\end{aligned}
\tag{4.12}
$$

What remains is the substitution of more fundamental functions for g_{t-1} and g_t.

Equation (2.13) gives an expression for dividend growth under conditions of complete certainty. However, under our present assumptions b, s, and r are constants and at any point in time the capitalization rate for that instant is also known. Therefore (2.13) may be rewritten with appropriate subscripts as

$$g_{t-1} = \frac{(b+s)r(1-b) - sk_{t-1}}{1-b-s}, 1 > b + s, \qquad (4.13)$$

and

$$g_t = \frac{(b+s)r(1-b) - sk_t}{1-b-s}, 1 > b + s. \qquad (4.14)$$

Substituting (4.13) and (4.14) into (4.12)

$$R_t = \frac{\left[k_{t-1} - \dfrac{(b+s)r(1-b) - sk_{t-1}}{1-b-s} \right](1+k_t)}{k_t - \dfrac{(b+s)r(1-b) - sk_t}{1-b-s}}$$

$$= \frac{(k_{t-1} - br - sr)(1+k_t)}{k_t - br - sr}; k_{t-1}, k_t > br + sr. \qquad (4.15)$$

Thus the holding period return relative may be written as

$$R_t = \frac{(k_{t-1} - ar)(1+k_t)}{k_t - ar}; k_{t-1}, k_t > ar; \qquad (4.16)$$

where

$$a = b + s \qquad (4.17)$$

is the rate of investment and financing as a fraction of earnings and ar is the rate of growth of total earnings and dividends. Finally the holding period return relative is expressed in terms of very fundamental corporate variables and we can derive its elasticity in terms of the capitalization rate.

By definition the absolute value of this capitalization rate elasticity is

$$\varepsilon(R,k) = \left| \frac{\partial R_t}{\partial k_t} \right| \cdot \frac{k_t}{R_t}$$

$$= \left| (k_{t-1} - ar) \left[\frac{1}{k_t - ar} - \frac{1 + k_t}{(k_t - ar)^2} \right] \right| \frac{k_t}{R_t}$$

$$= \left[\frac{(k_{t-1} - ar)(1 + ar)}{(k_t - ar)^2} \right] \frac{k_t(k_t - ar)}{(k_{t-1} - ar)(1 + k_t)}$$

$$= \frac{(1 + ar)k_t}{(k_t - ar)(1 + k_t)}, k_t > ar. \tag{4.18}$$

$\varepsilon(R,k)$ is a function of the capitalization rate and, by inspection, a positive function of ar, the growth rate of total earnings and dividends expected to be generated by the firm. This is confirmed by differentiating with respect to $\gamma = ar$. That is

$$\frac{\partial \varepsilon(R,k)}{\partial \gamma} = \frac{k_t}{(k_t - ar)(1 + k_t)} + \frac{(1 + ar)k_t}{(k_t - ar)^2(1 + k_t)}$$

$$= \frac{k_t}{(k_t - ar)^2}, k_t > ar.$$

$$> 0 \tag{4.19}$$

What this means, of course, is that given a small percentage change in the capitalization rate for dividends, the percentage change in the holding-period return is a positive function of the growth rate of total expected earnings and dividends as given by the product ar. If total expected earnings and dividends are growing rapidly a small unexpected change in the market capitalization rate will result in a relatively large unexpected change in the holding-period return relative, other things equal. However, we should be quick to say that we have not actually proved that the stock of rapidly growing firms will always have more volatile holding-period returns. It is well known by bond investors and students of bond markets that yields on short-term bonds fluctuate much more widely than yields on long-term bonds.[10] Therefore, it may also be the case that capitalization rates for dividends of slowly growing companies fluctuate more widely than those of rapidly growing companies. The question raised by our analysis is an empirical one. Nevertheless, our expectations are strong that the difference between the volatility of capitalization rates of companies growing at different rates is not sufficient to overcome what appears to be a strong tendency for rapidly growing firms to be more risky. Not only is the capitalization elasticity of holding-period returns a positive function of the corporate growth rate, but the second derivative with respect to growth is also positive. That is

$$\frac{\partial^2 \varepsilon(R,k)}{\partial \gamma^2} = \frac{2k_t}{(k_t - ar)^3}, k_t > ar. \tag{4.20}$$

The tendency for the elasticity of holding-period returns to increase with growth at an increasing rate adds to our conviction that capitalization risk is a positive function of growth.

One further paragraph may be useful here regarding the type of growth that our analysis indicates is important. In going from Equation (4.12) to (4.15) we lost the need to distinguish between retention and new equity financing for purposes of specifying the holding-period return relative. While this strengthens the case for the conjecture that dividend policy is irrelevant in perfectly competitive capital markets, it by no means proves the theorem. Not only are we operating under highly restrictive assumptions regarding the retention and stock financing rates, but we have also assumed that future earnings on net worth are perfectly certain. This, together with the fact that capitalization rates may fluctuate more widely for stocks with higher dividend payout rates, clearly prohibits drawing any conclusions regarding dividend policy at this point. However, it does seem that the growth of total expected dividends is a more relevant variable than the growth rate of dividends per share.

III. SYSTEMATIC CAPITALIZATION RISK

If we assume that capitalization rates for expected dividends are highly correlated among different stocks but that the correlation is not necessarily perfect we know that part of the holding-period capitalization risk for a given stock may be diversifiable according to the theory of Markowitz[11]. Therefore, the theory of capital asset prices originally developed by Sharpe[12] and Lintner[13] on the basis of Markowitz's earlier work is an appropriate frame of reference within which to proceed.

If all assets are traded in perfectly competitive capital markets by risk averse investors who have homogeneous beliefs, maximize expected utility on the basis of the first two moments of portfolio returns, and have access to a zero beta asset[14] it can be shown that the expected return on the jth stock is a function of its systematic or undiversifiable risk, β_{jt-1}, according to[15]

$$E_{t-1}(R_{jt}) = E_{t-1}(R_{ot}) + \beta_{jt-1} E_{t-1}(R_{mt} - R_{ot}). \qquad (4.21)$$

Here

$$E_{t-1}(R_{jt}) = \text{the expectation, at the end of period } t-1, \text{ of the holding-period return on stock } j \text{ to be realized at the end of period } t;$$

$$E_{t-1}(R_{mt}) = \text{the analogous expectation with respect to the holding period return on the market portfolio of stocks;}$$

$$E_{t-1}(R_{ot}) = \text{the expected return on the zero beta portfolio; and}$$

$$\beta_{jt-1} = \text{Cov}_{t-1}(R_{jt}, R_{mt})/\text{Var}_{t-1}(R_{mt}). \qquad (4.22)$$

If follows that we are interested in the role of corporate growth in determining the value of $\text{Cov}_{t-1}(R_{jt}, R_{mt})$.

If we assume that the expected dividends on the market portfolio grow forever according to the function

$$g_{mt} = \frac{(b_m + s_m)r_m(1 - b_m) - s_m k_{mt}}{1 - b_m - s_m}, b_m + s_m < 1, \qquad (4.23)$$

we can write

$$R_{mt} = \frac{(k_{mt-1} - a_m r_m)(1 + k_{mt})}{k_{mt} - a_m r_m}; k_{mt-1} > a_m r_m, k_{mt} > a_m r_m. \qquad (4.24)$$

This is analogous to (4.16) which may be subscripted to indicate the jth stock. Thus (4.16) and (4.24) may be substituted into the covariance expression $\text{Cov}_{t-1}(R_{jt}, R_{mt})$. However, the result may be overly difficult to interpret. A preferable procedure is to rearrange (4.16) and (4.24) by expanding the numerator and dividing through by the denominator. Thus, for (4.16)

$$R_{jt} = \frac{k_{jt-1} - a_j r_j + k_{jt} k_{jt-1} - k_{jt} a_j r_j}{k_{jt} - a_j r_j}$$

$$= 1 + k_{jt-1} + \frac{(1 + a_j r_j)(k_{jt-1} - k_{jt})}{k_{jt} - a_j r_j}; k_{jt-1}, k_{jt} > a_j r_j. \qquad (4.25)$$

Similarly,

$$R_{mt} = 1 + k_{mt-1} + \frac{(1 + a_m r_m)(k_{mt-1} - k_{mt})}{k_{mt} - a_m r_m}; k_{mt-1}, k_{mt} > a_m r_m. \qquad (4.26)$$

Since k_{jt-1}, k_{mt-1}, a_j, a_m, r_j, and r_m are not random variables the $1 + k_{jt-1}$ and $1 + k_{mt-1}$ terms disappear upon substitution into the covariance expression while $1 + a_j r_j$ and $1 + a_m r_m$ may be factored out. Accordingly,

$$\text{Cov}_{t-1}(R_{jt}, R_{mt}) = (1 + a_j r_j)(1 + a_m r_m)$$

$$\times \text{Cov}_{t-1}\left[\frac{k_{jt-1} - k_{jt}}{k_{jt} - a_j r_j}, \frac{k_{mt-1} - k_{mt}}{k_{mt} - a_m r_m}\right]. \qquad (4.27)$$

This is a significant result for the theory of finance. If k_{jt} and k_{mt} are positively correlated random variables, it is clear that the terms inside the covariance expression on the right of (4.27) are positively correlated. Moreover, $\text{Cov}_{t-1}(R_{jt}, R_{mt})$ appears to be a positive function of $a_j r_j$, the rate of growth of the jth company's expected total earnings and dividends. This may be seen merely by inspecting (4.27) or by differentiating with respect to $\gamma_j = a_j r_j$ under the null hypothesis that $f(k_{jt}, k_{mt})$, the joint probability density function of k_{jt} and k_{mt}, is independent of small changes in γ_j. Defining

$$h(k_{jt}, k_{mt}) = \left[\frac{k_{jt-1} - k_{jt}}{k_{jt} - \gamma_j} - E\left(\frac{k_{jt-1} - k_{jt}}{k_{jt} - \gamma_j}\right)\right]$$

$$\times \left[\frac{k_{mt-1} - k_{mt}}{k_{mt} - \gamma_m} - E\left(\frac{k_{mt-1} - k_{mt}}{k_{mt} - \gamma_m}\right)\right] \qquad (4.28)$$

equation (4.27) may be written

$$\text{Cov}_{t-1}(R_{jt}, R_{mt}) = (1 + \gamma_j)(1 + \gamma_m) \int\limits_{-\infty}^{\infty} \int\limits_{-\infty}^{\infty} h(k_{jt}, k_{mt}) f(k_{jt}, k_{mt})$$

$$\times \, dk_{jt} dk_{mt}. \tag{4.29}$$

Thus,[16] assuming $\partial \gamma_m / \partial \gamma_j = 0$ for simplicity,

$$\frac{\partial \text{Cov}_{t-1}(R_{jt}, R_{mt})}{\partial \gamma_j}$$

$$= (1 + \gamma_m) \int\limits_{-\infty}^{\infty} \int\limits_{-\infty}^{\infty} h(k_{jt}, k_{mt}) f(k_{jt}, k_{mt}) dk_{jt} dk_{mt}$$

$$+ (1 + \gamma_j)(1 + \gamma_m) \int\limits_{-\infty}^{\infty} \int\limits_{-\infty}^{\infty} h_{\gamma_j}(k_{jt}, k_{mt}) f(k_{jt}, k_{mt}) dk_{jt} dk_{mt} \tag{4.30}$$

where $h_{\gamma_j}(k_{jt}, k_{mt})$ is the partial derivative of $h(k_{jt}, k_{mt})$ with respect to γ_j. That is

$$h_{\gamma_j}(k_{jt}, k_{mt}) = \left[\frac{k_{jt-1} - k_{jt}}{(k_{jt} - \gamma_j)^2} - E\left(\frac{k_{jt-1} - k_{jt}}{(k_{jt} - \gamma_j)^2} \right) \right]$$

$$\times \left[\frac{k_{mt-1} - k_{mt}}{k_{mt} - \gamma_m} - E\left(\frac{k_{mt-1} - k_{mt}}{k_{mt} - \gamma_m} \right) \right]. \tag{4.31}$$

Substituting (4.28) and (4.31) into (4.30) we see that

$$\frac{\partial \text{Cov}_{t-1}(R_{jt}, R_{mt})}{\partial \gamma_j} = (1 + \gamma_m) \text{Cov}_{t-1} \left[\frac{k_{jt-1} - k_{jt}}{k_{jt} - \gamma_j}, \frac{k_{mt-1} - k_{mt}}{k_{mt} - \gamma_m} \right]$$

$$+ (1 + \gamma_j)(1 + \gamma_m) \text{Cov}_{t-1} \left[\frac{k_{jt-1} - k_{jt}}{(k_{jt} - \gamma_j)^2}, \frac{k_{mt-1} - k_{mt}}{k_{mt} - \gamma_m} \right]. \tag{4.32}$$

If k_{jt} and k_{mt} are positively correlated random variables, which is what we believe, while $-1 < \gamma_j < k_{jt}$ and $-1 < \gamma_m < k_{mt}$ from original convergence requirements, both terms on the right side of (4.32) are positive.

Under the null hypothesis that $f(k_{jt}, k_{mt})$ is independent of γ_j we have shown that $\text{Cov}_{t-1}(R_{jt}, R_{mt})$, or systematic capitalization risk, is a positive function of the growth rate of expected total earnings and dividends, $\gamma_j = a_j r_j$. We should be quick to point out, however, that the result means that the original null hypothesis under which the analysis was conducted is inconsistent with the result. Certainly if systematic capitalization risk is increased by an increase in $\gamma_j = a_j r_j$ it follows from the security market line (4.21) that at least the first moment of k_{jt} is also a positive function of γ_j. The question is whether or not this fact renders the result of the analysis useless. We don't believe it does. If the first moment of k_{jt} is a positive function of γ_j, which would seem to render our analysis incorrect, it is because an increase in γ_j causes the risk of the stock to increase. But this is the same result as before. Either way it must be true that an increase in γ_j *causes* the systematic risk of the stock to rise and all that is in doubt is the exact form of the function relating systematic risk to the value of γ_j.

In order to extend the analysis to a final result which shows the exact function referred to above for any stock two requirements must be met. First, the joint density function, $f(k_{jt}, k_{mt})$, must be specified. Second, the relationships between γ_j and the moments of k_{jt} and k_{mt} must be specified at the very least. While the first requirement is not impossible, the second one almost certainly is since it involves the solution to our basic problem concerning the relationship between $Cov_{t-1}(R_{jt}, R_{mt})$ and γ_j plus many additional factors. Therefore at this stage of the analysis we must be satisfied (if only temporarily) with establishing the theoretical basis for a hypothesis concerning the existence and sign of the relationship between the rate of growth of expected total corporate earnings and dividends, and the systematic capitalization risk of the common stock.

Chapter V

Growth and Systematic Risk:
Stochastic Earnings

I. INTRODUCTION

In the foregoing chapter we developed a theory of the relationship between corporate growth and the systematic capitalization risk of common stocks. There we assumed that the rate of return on corporate investment is known with certainty and is the same in every future period. The only source of risk in that theory is uncertainty associated with the capitalization rate that will be applied to expected future dividends by investors at the end of the current investment holding period. Having demonstrated a case for the hypothesis that systematic capitalization risk is a positive causal function of the rate of growth of total earnings and dividends we now move on to the task of gradually introducing more generality. In Sections II and III we assume that expectations for future returns on common equity follow an adaptive expectations model with adaptation coefficient equal to one. This assumption is motivated by our review of the literature on the dividend decision in Chapter III. Therefore,

$$\bar{r}_t = \lambda r_t + (1 - \lambda)\bar{r}_{t-1}, \tag{5.1}$$

where

$\bar{r}_t$ = expected return on net worth in periods $t + 1, t + 2, \ldots$;

r_t = actual return on net worth in period t; and

λ = the adaptation coefficient (assumed to equal one in Sections II and III).

Section II presents the elasticity of the investment holding-period return with respect to long-run profitability, and Section III extends the analysis in terms of the systematic risk of the Capital Asset Pricing Model. In Section IV we assume that the adaptive expectations model (5.1) has an adaptation coefficient between zero and one. This is the most general case considered and the most complex in terms of the derivation of the holding-period return model as well as its analysis in terms of the effect of corporate growth on systematic risk. The outcome of the analysis is support for the empirically testable hypothesis that systematic risk stemming both from uncertain earnings and from changing capitalization rates is a positive causal function of the rate of corporate growth from investment of equity regardless of its source.

II. ELASTICITY OF HOLDING-PERIOD RETURNS WITH RESPECT TO CHANGING LONG RUN PROFITABILITY

Our purpose in this section is to examine the effects of changes in the long-run profitability of a company on the holding-period return on its common stock with a view to determining the role played by corporate growth in attenuating or magnifying those effects. Since we are interested in long-run profitability specifically, we will temporarily ignore changes in profits which are not expected to continue into the future by assuming that all changes are expected to be permanent on average. This is accomplished by assuming that the expected rate of return on common equity for the future is always equal to the rate of return on common equity realized in the most recent holding period.

Following our earlier convention the holding-period return for a common stock is given by

$$R_t = \frac{1}{P_{t-1}}(D_t + P_t) \qquad (5.2)$$

where we assume that the share prices are given by

$$P_t = \frac{E_t(D_{t+1})}{k_t - g_t}, k_t > g_t, \qquad (5.3)$$

and

$$P_{t-1} = \frac{E_{t-1}(D_t)}{k_{t-1} - g_{t-1}}, k_{t-1} > g_{t-1}, \qquad (5.4)$$

at the end of periods t and t − 1, respectively. If the common equity at the end of period t is denoted by A_t and if $\bar{r}_t$ is the rate of return expected on common equity in every period from t + 1 onward, it must be true that the expected dividend in (5.3) is given by

$$E_t(D_{t+1}) = A_t \bar{r}_t(1 - b). \qquad (5.5)$$

Therefore, equation (5.3) may be rewritten as

$$P_t = \frac{A_t \bar{r}_t(1 - b)}{k_t - g_t}, k_t > g_t, \qquad (5.6)$$

and similarly,

$$P_{t-1} = \frac{A_{t-1} \bar{r}_{t-1}(1 - b)}{k_{t-1} - g_{t-1}}, k_{t-1} > g_{t-1}. \qquad (5.7)$$

However, the actual dividend paid in period t must be determined either by the actual profit realized or possibly by expectations of future corporate profitability as at the end of period t. Under our assumptions, these are identical so that

$$\begin{aligned} D_t &= A_{t-1} r_t(1 - b) \\ &= A_{t-1} \bar{r}_t(1 - b). \end{aligned} \qquad (5.8)$$

Substituting (5.6), (5.7) and (5.8) into (5.2)

$$R_t = \frac{1}{\left[\dfrac{A_{t-1}\bar{r}_{t-1}(1-b)}{k_{t-1}-g_{t-1}}\right]} \left[A_{t-1}\bar{r}_{t-1}(1-b) + \frac{A_t\bar{r}_t(1-b)}{k_t-g_t}\right]$$

$$= \left[\frac{(k_{t-1}-g_{t-1})\bar{r}_t}{A_{t-1}\bar{r}_{t-1}}\right]\left[A_{t-1} + \frac{A_t}{k_t-g_t}\right], k_t > g_t, k_{t-1} > g_{t-1}.$$

$$(5.9)$$

Further simplification is possible if A_t is expressed in terms of A_{t-1} and g_t. In what follows we assume that the growth rate of expected dividends is adequately approximated by

$$g_t = \frac{(b+s)\bar{r}_t(1-b) - sk_t}{1-b-s}, b+s < 1, \qquad (5.10)$$

which Miller and Modigliani[1] have shown holds exactly when the return on net worth is certain and equal to a constant in every future period and which also holds exactly when future deviations of returns on net worth from $\bar{r}_t$ are serially independent. In any case, since g_{t-1} appears in the denominator and g_t appears in the numerator of (5.9) the error in using (5.10) as an exact expression is minimal.

If the firm retains the fraction b of its earnings for reinvestment and raises new equity equal to the fraction s of its earnings each period the *total* common equity of the firm will grow during period t at the rate $br_t + sr_t$. However, common equity *per share* will grow at a lesser rate due to the increase in shares outstanding. Gordon has shown that because new equity is invested to earn an expected return $\bar{r}_t$ while new shareholders require the rate k_t, a fraction v_t of the new issue accrues to the benefit of shareholders of record prior to the new issue.[2] Thus the rate of increase in common equity per share during period t is equal to $b\bar{r}_t + s\bar{r}_t v_t$. Since v_t is given by[3]

$$v_t = \frac{\bar{r}_t - k_t}{\bar{r}_t(1-b-s)}, b+s < 1, \qquad (5.11)$$

the rate of growth in common equity per share during period t is

(*ex post*)

$$b\bar{r}_t + s\bar{r}_t\left[\frac{\bar{r}_t - k_t}{\bar{r}_t(1 - b - s)}\right] = \frac{(b + s)\bar{r}_t(1 - b) - sk_t}{1 - b - s}$$

$$= g_t. \qquad (5.12)$$

Therefore we can write

$$A_t = A_{t-1}(1 + g_t) \qquad (5.13)$$

and substituting for A_t in (5.9)

$$R_t = \left[\frac{(k_{t-1} - g_{t-1})\bar{r}_t}{A_{t-1}\bar{r}_{t-1}}\right]\left[\frac{A_{t-1}(1 + g_t)}{k_t - g_t}\right]$$

$$= \frac{(k_{t-1} - g_{t-1})\bar{r}_t(1 + k_t)}{\bar{r}_{t-1}(k_t - g_t)}, k_{t-1} > g_{t-1}, k_t > g_t. \qquad (5.14)$$

Employing (5.10) for g_t

$$k_t - g_t = k_t - \frac{(b + s)\bar{r}_t(1 - b) - sk_t}{1 - b - s}$$

$$= \frac{(k_t - b\bar{r}_t - s\bar{r}_t)(1 - b)}{1 - b - s}$$

$$= \frac{(k_t - a\bar{r}_t)(1 - b)}{1 - a} \qquad (5.15)$$

where $a = b + s < 1$.
Similarly,

$$k_{t-1} - g_{t-1} = \frac{(k_{t-1} - a\bar{r}_{t-1})(1 - b)}{1 - a}, a < 1. \qquad (5.16)$$

Substituting (5.15) and (5.16) into (5.14) we finally obtain the holding-period return in terms of a very fundamental set of corporate variables. That is

$$R_t = \frac{(k_{t-1} - a\bar{r}_{t-1})\bar{r}_t(1 + k_t)}{\bar{r}_{t-1}(k_t - a\bar{r}_t)}, a < 1, \qquad (5.17)$$

$k_{t-1} < a\bar{r}_{t-1}$, and $k_t < a\bar{r}_t$.

The elasticity of R_t with respect to $\bar{r}_t$ is one measure of the volatility of the holding-period return of a stock with respect to changes in long-run profitability of the company's equity investments. This elasticity is given by

$$\varepsilon(R_t, \bar{r}_t) = \frac{\partial R_t}{\partial \bar{r}_t} \cdot \frac{\bar{r}_t}{R_t}$$

$$= \left[\frac{(k_{t-1} - a\bar{r}_{t-1})(1 + k_t)}{\bar{r}_{t-1}} \right] \left[\frac{1}{k_t - a\bar{r}_t} + \frac{a\bar{r}_t}{(k_t - a\bar{r}_t)^2} \right] \frac{\bar{r}_t}{R_t}$$

$$= \frac{(k_{t-1} - a\bar{r}_{t-1})(1 + k_t)k_t\bar{r}_t}{\bar{r}_{t-1}(k_t - a\bar{r}_t)^2} \cdot \frac{\bar{r}_{t-1}(k_{t-1} - a\bar{r}_{t-1})}{(k_{t-1} - a\bar{r}_{t-1})\bar{r}_t(1 + k_t)}$$

$$= \frac{k_t}{k_t - a\bar{r}_t}, k_t > a\bar{r}_t. \tag{5.18}$$

The elasticity is a positive function of the rate of growth of total earnings and dividends. Differentiating with respect to the rate of total equity investment

$$\frac{\partial \varepsilon(R_t, \bar{r}_t)}{\partial a} = \frac{k_t\bar{r}_t}{(k_t - a\bar{r}_t)^2} > 0, k_t > a\bar{r}_t. \tag{5.19}$$

Any change in long-run profitability has an effect on the holding-period return that is magnified by the rate at which the company invests retained earnings and new equity with no distinction necessary as to the proportion of financing obtained from each source.

The size of $\bar{r}_t$ for a company is only one of several measures of its expected long run profitability. Perhaps a more meaningful statistic is an index of $\bar{r}_t$ relative to k_t. If we define

$$z_t = \bar{r}_t/k_t, k_t > 0, \tag{5.20}$$

then any change in either $\bar{r}_t$ or in k_t shows up in z_t. Substituting

$$\bar{r}_t = z_t k_t \tag{5.21}$$

and

$$\bar{r}_{t-1} = z_{t-1} k_{t-1} \tag{5.22}$$

into the expression for the holding-period return (5.17)

$$R_t = \frac{(1 - az_{t-1})(1 + k_t)z_t}{(1 - az_t)z_{t-1}}, az_{t-1} \text{ and } az_t < 1, z_{t-1} > 0. \quad (5.23)$$

The elasticity of R_t with respect to z_t is given by

$$
\begin{aligned}
\varepsilon(R_t, z_t) &= \frac{\partial R_t}{\partial z_t} \cdot \frac{z_t}{R_t} \\
&= \left[\frac{1 - az_{t-1}}{z_{t-1}} \right]\left[\frac{1 + k_t + z_t dk_t/dz_t}{1 - az_t} + \frac{az_t(1 + k_t)}{(1 - az_t)^2} \right] \\
&\quad \times \frac{z_t(1 - az_t)z_{t-1}}{(1 - az_{t-1})(1 + k_t)z_t} \\
&= \frac{1}{1 - az_t} + \frac{z_t dk_t/dz_t}{1 + k_t}, az_t < 1, \quad (5.24)
\end{aligned}
$$

and it is a positive function of the rate of corporate investment. That is,

$$\frac{\partial \varepsilon(R_t, z_t)}{\partial a} = \frac{z_t}{(1 - az_t)^2} > 0, az_t < 1, \text{ and } z_t > 0. \quad (5.25)$$

To summarize this section, we have derived the function for the holding-period return on a stock with constant expected dividend growth under the assumption that expectations of long-run profitability are fully adaptive to changes in current profitability. We then examined the elasticity of the holding-period return with respect to two measures of long-run profitability; return on net worth, and return on net worth as a fraction of the capitalization rate for expected dividends. Both elasticities are positive functions of the rate of corporate investment of equity whether from retained earnings or from new equity issues.

III. CHANGING PROFITABILITY AND SYSTEMATIC RISK

From the foregoing it is clear that we have a case for hypothesizing that the volatility of holding-period returns on a stock is a positive causal function of the growth rate of total company earnings and dividends brought about by equity investment. Moreover, if we think of the long run profitability of a company's net worth as positively correlated with the long run profitability of the net worth of the market portfolio it is clear that the systematic or undiversifiable risk due to changing profitability may also be a positive causal function of corporate growth. Therefore it is of some interest to examine the relationships concerned.

Under the assumptions of Section II the holding period return on a stock is given by equation (5.17). In examining the systematic or undiversifiable effect of changes in the expected return on net worth we can conveniently assume away changes in the capitalization rate over time. Then (5.17) may be written without the time subscript on k. Adding subscripts j and m to denote variables corresponding to the jth stock and the market portfolio of stocks, respectively, we can write

$$\text{Cov}_{t-1}(R_{jt}, R_{mt}) = \text{Cov}_{t-1}\left[\frac{(k_j - a_j \bar{r}_{jt-1})\bar{r}_{jt}(1 + k_j)}{(k_j - a_j \bar{r}_{jt})\bar{r}_{jt-1}}, \frac{(k_m - a_m \bar{r}_{mt-1})\bar{r}_{mt}(1 + k_m)}{(k_m - a_m \bar{r}_{mt})\bar{r}_{mt-1}}\right]. \quad (5.26)$$

If we assume the null hypothesis that k_j is independent of a_j and also assume that a change in a_j has no effect on the joint distribution of $\bar{r}_{jt}$ and $\bar{r}_{mt}$, we can differentiate (5.26) with respect to a_j. Note that we are employing a partial equilibrium analysis in that we assume that all market portfolio variables are independent of a_j. Differentiating

$$\frac{\partial \text{Cov}_{t-1}(R_{jt}, R_{mt})}{\partial a_j}$$

$$= \text{Cov}_{t-1}\left[\frac{\bar{r}_{jt}(1 + k_j)}{\bar{r}_{jt-1}}\left(\frac{(k_j - a_j \bar{r}_{jt-1})\bar{r}_{jt}}{(k_j - a_j \bar{r}_{jt})^2} - \frac{\bar{r}_{jt-1}}{k_j - a_j \bar{r}_{jt}}\right),\right.$$

$$\left.\frac{(k_m - a_m \bar{r}_{mt-1})\bar{r}_{mt}(1 + k_m)}{(k_m - a_m \bar{r}_{mt})\bar{r}_{mt-1}}\right]$$

$$= \text{Cov}_{t-1}\left[\frac{\bar{r}_{jt}(1 + k_j)k_j(\bar{r}_{jt} - \bar{r}_{jt-1})}{\bar{r}_{jt-1}(k_j - a_j \bar{r}_{jt})^2}, \frac{(k_m - a_m \bar{r}_{mt-1})\bar{r}_{mt}(1 + k_m)}{(k_m - a_m \bar{r}_{mt})\bar{r}_{mt-1}}\right].$$

$$(5.27)$$

Noting that $\bar{r}_{jt}$ and $\bar{r}_{mt}$ are the only random variables in (5.27) we can factor out terms that are not stochastic. Thus

$$\frac{\partial \text{Cov}_{t-1}(R_{jt}, R_{mt})}{\partial a_j} = \frac{(1 + k_j)k_j(k_m - a_m\bar{r}_{mt-1})(1 + k_m)}{\bar{r}_{jt-1}\,\bar{r}_{mt-1}}$$

$$\times \text{Cov}_{t-1}\left[\frac{\bar{r}_{jt}(\bar{r}_{jt} - \bar{r}_{jt-1})}{(k_j - a_j\bar{r}_{jt})^2}, \frac{\bar{r}_{mt}}{k_m - a_m\bar{r}_{mt}}\right]. \quad (5.28)$$

Provided $\bar{r}_{jt}$ and $\bar{r}_{mt}$ are positively correlated it is obvious from inspection of (5.28) that the covariance term on the right-hand side is positive. Moreover, for a positive finite share price under our model assumptions, the terms preceding the covariance terms are also all positive meaning that the derivative of $\text{Cov}_{t-1}(R_{jt}, R_{mt})$ with respect to a_j, the rate of investment by firm j, is positive. Systematic risk arising from changes in long run profitability as measured by $\bar{r}_{jt}$ appears to be a positive function of the rate of corporate growth whether the equity invested is raised from retained earnings or new stock issue.

However, as discussed in Section II, $\bar{r}_{jt}$ is only one way of describing long-run profitability. A more meaningful measure of long-run profitability expectations requires a comparison of $\bar{r}_{jt}$ with k_{jt}. Employing the definition introduced in Section II,

$$z_{jt} = \bar{r}_{jt}/k_{jt}, k_{jt} > 0, \quad (5.29)$$

the holding-period return may be written as in (5.23) above. Noting that

$$(1 + k_t)z_t = \bar{r}_t + z_t, \quad (5.30)$$

equation (5.23) changes to

$$R_t = \frac{(1 - az_{t-1})(\bar{r}_t + z_t)}{z_{t-1}(1 - az_t)}, az_{t-1} \text{ and } az_t < 1, z_{t-1} > 0. \quad (5.31)$$

Adding subscripts to denote the jth stock and the market portfolio,

$$\text{Cov}_{t-1}(R_{jt}, R_{mt}) = \text{Cov}_{t-1}\left[\frac{(1 - a_j z_{jt-1})(\bar{r}_{jt} + z_{jt})}{z_{jt-1}(1 - a_j z_{jt})},\right.$$

$$\left.\frac{(1 - a_m z_{mt-1})(\bar{r}_{mt} + z_{mt})}{z_{mt-1}(1 - a_m z_{mt})}\right]. \quad (5.32)$$

Differentiating this expression with respect to a_j will indicate the role of corporate growth when $\bar{r}_{jt}$, k_{jt}, $\bar{r}_{mt}$ and k_{mt} are assumed to be stochastic.

Under the null hypothesis that the joint distribution of k_{jt}, k_{mt}, $\bar{r}_{jt}$ and $\bar{r}_{mt}$ is independent of a_j, as is a_m, the derivative of (5.32) with respect to a_j is given by

$$\frac{\partial \text{Cov}_{t-1}(R_{jt}, R_{mt})}{\partial a_j} = \text{Cov}_{t-1}\left[\frac{(z_{jt} - z_{jt-1})(\bar{r}_{jt} + z_{jt})}{z_{jt-1}(1 - a_j z_{jt})^2}, \right.$$

$$\left. \frac{(1 - a_m z_{mt-1})(\bar{r}_{mt} + z_{mt})}{z_{mt-1}(1 - a_m z_{mt})} \right]. \quad (5.33)$$

Factoring out the terms which are not stochastic

$$\frac{\partial \text{Cov}_{t-1}(R_{jt}, R_{mt})}{\partial a_j} = \frac{(1 - a_m z_{mt-1})}{z_{jt-1} z_{mt-1}}$$

$$\times \text{Cov}_{t-1}\left[\frac{(z_{jt} - z_{jt-1})(\bar{r}_{jt} + z_{jt})}{(1 - a_j z_{jt})^2}, \frac{(\bar{r}_{mt} + z_{mt})}{(1 - a_m z_{mt})}\right]. \quad (5.34)$$

If we assume that $\bar{r}_{jt}$, $\bar{r}_{mt}$, z_{jt} and z_{mt} are positively correlated it is clear that the covariance term on the right hand side of (5.34) is is positive. It may be positive under an even weaker but more complex assumption. In any case, the positive covariance term together with the positive term preceding it indicates that $\text{Cov}_{t-1}(R_{jt}, R_{mt})$ is a positive function of the rate of corporate equity investment when systematic risk stems from uncertainty in all four variables, k_{jt}, k_{mt}, $\bar{r}_{jt}$ and $\bar{r}_{mt}$.

Once again (see Chapter IV) we are presented with an inconsistency between the earlier assumption that the joint distribution of k_{jt}, k_{mt}, $\bar{r}_{jt}$ and $\bar{r}_{mt}$ is independent of a_j, and the result which indicates that the stock is riskier as a_j increases so that at least the first moment of k_{jt} must be a positive function of a_j. All we can do is say that while the analysis becomes intractable without the earlier assumption, the basic conclusion that stock risk increases with a_j is sound. What we are forced to forgo is a derivation of the exact form of the causal relationship between a_j and $Cov_{t-1}(R_{jt}, R_{mt})$ while we are left with the hypothesis that the function exists and is positive in sign.

IV. PARTIALLY ADAPTIVE EXPECTATIONS

In the preceding section we assumed that whatever the return on common equity is during the holding period for a stock, the expected future return on common equity adapts fully to that value in the minds of investors. There is no doubt that current earnings usually carry important information about future prospects but it is also undoubtedly true that investors may discount changes in current earnings as being indicative of somewhat smaller changes in expected future earnings per dollar of common equity. This is consistent with a model of expectations such as (5.1). That is

$$\bar{r}_t = \lambda r_t + (1 - \lambda)\bar{r}_{t-1}, 0 < \lambda < 1. \qquad (5.35)$$

Under this description of the formation of expectations regarding future profitability there is a second question that must be resolved concerning dividend policy. That is, if the current return on net worth is different from the return that is expected in subsequent periods, what is a suitable model with which to describe the dividend decision? Are dividends paid on the basis of past levels, on the basis of current profits in each period, on the basis of expected future profitability, or on the basis of something else? The question is a difficulty one and has been the subject of our review of the literature which followed Lintner's seminal work.[4]

One view of dividend policy is that dividends contain considerable information concerning the expectations of management with respect to future profitability. In our review we concluded that this view has never been adequately tested. We also found that dividends are paid according to a partial adjustment model where the change from a previous dividend level toward an "ideal" level, based on management expectations of future profits, is only partial. This partial adjustment model is difficult to use in what follows but it has the same reduced form as a partial adaptation model of expected profits which is easier to employ.[5] Consequently, we assume in what follows that dividends are paid according to a stable fraction, $1 - b$, of the earnings that would have been realized in the holding period concerned had the rate of return on common equity been equal to the expected return for future periods. That is, if A_{t-1} is the common equity per share at the start of period t, the dividend per share in period t is equal to

$$D_t = A_{t-1}\bar{r}_t(1 - b) \tag{5.36}$$

where $\bar{r}_t$ is determined according to (5.35). Accordingly, the expected value of D_t as of the end of period $t - 1$ is

$$
\begin{aligned}
E_{t-1}(D_t) &= E_{t-1}[A_{t-1}\bar{r}_t(1 - b)] \\
&= A_{t-1}E_{t-1}[\lambda r_t + (1 - \lambda)\bar{r}_{t-1}](1 - b) \\
&= A_{t-1}\bar{r}_{t-1}(1 - b) \tag{5.37}
\end{aligned}
$$

and the stock price is

$$
\begin{aligned}
P_{t-1} &= \frac{E_{t-1}(D_t)}{k_{t-1} - g_{t-1}} \\
&= \frac{A_{t-1}\bar{r}_{t-1}(1 - b)}{k_{t-1} - g_{t-1}}, k_{t-1} > g_{t-1}. \tag{5.38}
\end{aligned}
$$

Similarly,

$$P_t = \frac{A_t\bar{r}_t(1 - b)}{k_t - g_t}, k_t > g_t. \tag{5.39}$$

Substituting (5.36), (5.38) and (5.39) into (5.2) gives

$$
\begin{aligned}
R_t &= \frac{(k_{t-1} - g_{t-1})}{A_{t-1}\bar{r}_{t-1}(1 - b)}\left[A_{t-1}\bar{r}_t(1 - b) + \frac{A_t\bar{r}_t(1 - b)}{k_t - g_t}\right] \\
&= \frac{(k_{t-1} - g_{t-1})\bar{r}_t}{A_{t-1}\bar{r}_{t-1}}\left[\frac{A_{t-1}(k_t - g_t) + A_t}{k_t - g_t}\right]. \tag{5.40}
\end{aligned}
$$

The next step requires a convenient notational definition, the purpose of which will become clear later in the analysis.

Let θ_t be defined as the rate at which common equity grows during period t *in excess* of the rate of growth of dividend expectations from period t onward. That is, let θ_t be defined such that the following equality holds:

$$A_t = A_{t-1}(1 + g_t + \theta_t).\tag{5.41}$$

Then substituting (5.41) into (5.40)

$$R_t = \frac{(k_{t-1} - g_{t-1})\bar{r}_t(1 + k_t + \theta_t)}{(k_t - g_t)\bar{r}_{t-1}}.\tag{5.42}$$

Substituting (5.10) for g_t and g_{t-1},

$$R_t = \frac{(k_{t-1} - a\bar{r}_{t-1})\bar{r}_t(1 + k_t + \theta_t)}{(k_t - a\bar{r}_t)\bar{r}_{t-1}},\tag{5.43}$$

where $a = b + s$, the rate of equity investment as a fraction of the earnings that would have been realized had the actual rate of return on common equity in period $t - 1$ and period t been equal to $\bar{r}_{t-1}$ and $\bar{r}_t$, respectively.

At this point θ_t is the only variable in equation (5.43) which is not a fundamental corporate variable. Therefore we turn to the derivation of the expression with which to replace it.

If dividends are paid according to equation (5.36) and if actual earnings per share in period t are given by

$$Y_t = A_{t-1}r_t,\tag{5.44}$$

the earnings retained are equal to

$$Y_t - D_t = A_{t-1}r_t - A_{t-1}\bar{r}_t(1 - b).\tag{5.45}$$

However, if the total equity investment at the end of period t is equal to the fraction $a = b + s$ of the earnings that would have been realized if the return on common equity had been $\bar{r}_t$ then the amount invested per share is

$$I_t = (b + s)A_{t-1}\bar{r}_t.\tag{5.46}$$

Accordingly, the amount of new equity to be issued per share already outstanding is

$$\begin{aligned}
q_t &= I_t - (Y_t - D_t) \\
&= (b + s)A_{t-1}\bar{r}_t - [A_{t-1}r_t - A_{t-1}\bar{r}_t(1 - b)] \\
&= A_{t-1}[\bar{r}_t(1 + s) - r_t]
\end{aligned}\tag{5.47}$$

and the equity accretion per share is equal to

$$v_t q_t = v_t A_{t-1} [\bar{r}_t(1+s) - r_t]. \tag{5.48}$$

Now we are in a position to relate A_t to A_{t-1} and infer the expression for θ_t by referring to the defining equation (5.41). Since retained earnings per share are given by $Y_t - D_t$ and equity accretion per share by $v_t q_t$ we have

$$
\begin{aligned}
A_t &= A_{t-1} + (Y_t - D_t) + v_t q_t \\
&= A_{t-1} + [A_{t-1} r_t - A_{t-1} \bar{r}_t(1-b)] + v_t A_{t-1} [r_t(1+s) - r_t] \\
&= A_{t-1} [1 + b\bar{r}_t + s\bar{r}_t v_t + (1 - v_t)(r_t - \bar{r}_t)]. \tag{5.49}
\end{aligned}
$$

If the return on common equity had been equal to $\bar{r}_t$ in period t (i.e. $r_t = \bar{r}_t$) the common equity per share would have grown at the rate g_t. Consequently, comparing (5.49) with (5.41)

$$g_t = b\bar{r}_t + s\bar{r}_t v_t \tag{5.50}$$

and

$$\theta_t = (1 - v_t)(r_t - \bar{r}_t). \tag{5.51}$$

Equating (5.50) with (5.10) we can solve for v_t. That is,

$$b\bar{r}_t + s\bar{r}_t v_t = \frac{(b+s)\bar{r}_t(1-b) - sk_t}{1 - b - s} \tag{5.52}$$

and solving,

$$v_t = \frac{\bar{r}_t - k_t}{\bar{r}_t(1 - b - s)}. \tag{5.53}$$

This agrees with the similar expression for the equity accretion rate originally derived by Gordon using a slightly different definition for the rate of outside financing.[6]
  Substituting (5.53) for v_t in (5.51)

$$\theta_t = \frac{(r_t - \bar{r}_t)(k_t - a\bar{r}_t)}{\bar{r}_t(1 - a)} \tag{5.54}$$

where $a = b + s$ as before. Now we can substitute for θ_t in the equation for holding period return (5.43) to obtain

$$R_t = \frac{(k_{t-1} - a\bar{r}_{t-1})\bar{r}_t}{(k_t - a\bar{r}_t)\bar{r}_{t-1}}\left[1 + k_t + \frac{(r_t - \bar{r}_t)(k_t - a\bar{r}_t)}{\bar{r}_t(1-a)}\right]$$

$$= \frac{(k_{t-1} - a\bar{r}_{t-1})(1+k_t)\bar{r}_t}{(k_t - a\bar{r}_t)\bar{r}_{t-1}} + \frac{(k_{t-1} - a\bar{r}_{t-1})(r_t - \bar{r}_t)}{\bar{r}_{t-1}(1-a)} \quad (5.55)$$

Since by (5.35)

$$r_t - \bar{r}_t = r_t - \lambda r_t + (1-\lambda)\bar{r}_{t-1}$$
$$= (1-\lambda)(r_{t-1} - \bar{r}_{t-1}) \quad (5.56)$$

we can write

$$R_t = \frac{(k_{t-1} - a\bar{r}_{t-1})\bar{r}_t(1+k_t)}{(k_t - a\bar{r}_t)\bar{r}_{t-1}} + \frac{(k_{t-1} - a\bar{r}_{t-1})(1-\lambda)(r_t - \bar{r}_{t-1})}{\bar{r}_{t-1}(1-a)} \quad (5.57)$$

The first term of (5.57) is identical to equation (5.17) and the second term is stochastic in r_t alone. Employing

$$z_t = \bar{r}_t / k_t \quad (5.58)$$

the first term becomes identical to (5.31) and

$$R_t = \frac{(1 - az_{t-1})(\bar{r}_t + z_t)}{z_{t-1}(1 - az_t)} + \frac{(1 - az_{t-1})(1-\lambda)(r_t - \bar{r}_{t-1})}{z_{t-1}(1-a)} \quad (5.59)$$

This expression for R_t is amenable to analysis in terms of systematic risk. Subscripting to denote the jth stock and the market portfolio of stocks, the covariance of R_{jt} and R_{mt} may be expressed as

$$\text{Cov}_{t-1}(R_{jt}, R_{mt})$$

$$= \text{Cov}_{t-1}\left[\frac{(1 - a_j z_{jt-1})(\bar{r}_{jt} + z_{jt})}{z_{jt-1}(1 - a_j z_{jt})}, \frac{(1 - a_m z_{mt-1})(\bar{r}_{mt} + z_{mt})}{z_{mt-1}(1 - a_m z_{mt})}\right]$$

$$+ \text{Cov}_{t-1}\left[\frac{(1 - a_j z_{jt-1})(\bar{r}_{jt} + z_{jt})}{z_{jt-1}(1 - a_j z_{jt})}, \frac{(1 - a_m z_{mt-1})(1-\lambda_m)r_{mt}}{z_{mt-1}(1-a_m)}\right]$$

$$+ \text{Cov}_{t-1}\left[\frac{(1 - a_j z_{jt-1})(1-\lambda_j)r_{jt}}{z_{jt-1}(1-a_j)}, \frac{(1 - a_m z_{mt-1})(\bar{r}_{mt} + z_{mt})}{z_{mt-1}(1 - a_m z_{mt})}\right]$$

$$+ \text{Cov}_{t-1}\left[\frac{(1 - a_j z_{jt-1})(1-\lambda_j)r_{jt}}{z_{jt-1}(1-a_j)}, \frac{(1 - a_m z_{mt-1})(1-\lambda_m)r_{mt}}{z_{mt-1}(1-a_m)}\right].$$

$$(5.60)$$

If we assume that a_m is independent of a_j and that a_j doesn't affect the joint probability distribution of r_{jt}, z_{jt}, r_{mt} and z_{mt}; the partial derivative of $\text{Cov}_{t-1}(R_{jt}, R_{mt})$ with respect to a_j is given by

$$\frac{\partial \text{Cov}_{t-1}(R_{jt}, R_{mt})}{\partial a_j}$$

$$= \frac{(1 - a_m z_{mt-1})}{z_{jt-1} z_{mt-1}} \text{Cov}_{t-1}\left[\frac{(z_{jt} - z_{jt-1})(\bar{r}_{jt} + z_{jt})}{(1 - a_j z_{jt})^2}, \frac{(\bar{r}_{mt} + z_{mt})}{(1 - a_m z_{mt})} \right]$$

$$+ \frac{(1 - a_m z_{mt-1})(1 - \lambda_m)}{z_{jt-1} z_{mt-1}(1 - a_m)} \text{Cov}_{t-1}\left[\frac{(z_{jt} - z_{jt-1})(\bar{r}_{jt} + z_{jt})}{(1 - a_j z_{jt})^2}, r_{mt} \right]$$

$$+ \frac{(1 - z_{jt-1})(1 - \lambda_j)(1 - a_m z_{mt-1})}{z_{jt-1}(1 - a_j)^2 z_{mt-1}} \text{Cov}_{t-1}\left[r_{jt}, \frac{(\bar{r}_{mt} + z_{mt})}{(1 - a_m z_{mt})} \right]$$

$$+ \frac{(1 - z_{jt-1})(1 - \lambda_j)(1 - \lambda_m)(1 - a_m z_{mt-1})}{z_{jt-1}(1 - a_j)^2 z_{mt-1}(1 - a_m)} \text{Cov}_{t-1}[r_{jt}, r_{mt}].$$

$$(5.61)$$

The first term in (5.61) is identical with the right-hand side of equation (5.34) and was discussed there. Specifically, the first term is positive under the plausible condition that $\bar{r}_{jt}, z_{jt}, \bar{r}_{mt}$ and z_{mt} are all positively correlated. The last three terms are added to that of (5.34) as a result of the more general assumption here that investor expectations concerning future returns on net worth are only partly adaptive to changes in the return on net worth in the current period from what was expected. If $\bar{r}_{jt}$ and z_{jt} are positively correlated with r_{mt} the second term is positive, since $\dfrac{(z_{jt} - z_{jt-1})(\bar{r}_{jt} + z_{jt})}{(1 - a_j z_{jt})^2}$ is a positive function of both $\bar{r}_{jt}$ and z_{jt}, while conditions required for positive finite share prices dictate that the term in front of the covariance is positive if $0 < \lambda_m < 1$. As for the third and fourth terms, the covariances are positive as long as r_{jt} is positively correlated with r_{mt}, $\bar{r}_{mt}$ and z_{mt}, which is very likely true for most companies. However, both covariances are multiplied by the term $1 - z_{jt-1}$ which is positive only when $\bar{r}_{jt-1} < k_{jt-1}$.

That condition is *not* likely to hold up in general and we would expect it to be violated much of the time, especially for rapidly growing companies in industries where investment opportunities are lucrative. The condition can only be expected to hold when equity capital is invested to earn less than its cost or, in other words, when the market value of equity falls below its book value. Our analysis has clearly left us with an uncertain result. The sign of the effect of corporate growth on systematic stock risk will depend upon which terms in equation (5.61) are dominant. We strongly suspect that the first two terms are by far the most important because they deal with long-term profitability changes which by their nature have more effect on holding period returns than do temporary fluctuations in the current return on net worth. However, the question can only be further resolved with recourse to empirical research.

V. SUMMARY

In this chapter we have extended our earlier analysis of the relationship between corporate growth and common stock risk to include the case of uncertain earnings. Initially we assumed that unanticipated changes in realized return on common equity are expected to continue in the future and found that both the elasticity of holding period returns with respect to long run profitability and the systematic risk of capital asset pricing theory are positive functions of the rate of total corporate equity investment whether financed from retained earnings or from new equity issue. This result holds, whether long run profitability is defined in terms of the rate of return on common equity alone or in terms of the rate of return on common equity divided by the capitalization rate for expected dividends. This last statistic allows us to treat both the return on common equity and the capitalization rate as stochastic variables simultaneously in the analysis.

Endeavoring to make the result more general, we then relaxed the assumption that all unanticipated changes in return on common equity are expected to continue in the future in favor of a more general assumption that return on net worth expectations are formed according to an adaptive expectations model with only partial adaptation. This may accurately reflect the reluctance of investors to give full weight to single observations of changes in earnings levels in forming their expectations for the future. With this change we were able to derive function (5.59) for holding-period returns that is expressed in two terms, one of which contains only long-run profitability expectations as its stochastic variable and the other of which contains only the rate of return on common equity during the holding period concerned as its stochastic variable. The subsequent analysis of the effect of corporate growth on systematic risk stemming from these variables indicates that the risk stemming from changes in long run profitability expectations, as measured by the expected return on common equity divided by the capitalization rate for expected dividends, is a positive function of the rate of total corporate equity investment while the risk stemming from uncertainty in the return to be realized on common equity *during* the holding period is either a positive or negative function of total corporate equity investment depending upon whether the return on common equity, $\bar{r}_{jt-1}$, is less than or greater than the capitalization rate, k_{jt-1}, respectively. Table 5.1 provides a more complete and precise summary of the outcome. The first column shows overall systematic risk in terms of the two basic types of uncertainty involved in holding a stock, the second column shows that the effect of corporate growth on systematic risk from either source is positive when the expectation at the *start* of the holding period is that the future return on net worth will be less then the capitalization rate for future dividends. The third column presents the case where expected return on com-

Table 5.1. Effect of Corporate Growth on the Systematic Risk of Stocks

Source of Risk (Random Variable)	$\bar{r}_{jt-1} < k_{jt-1}$	$\bar{r}_{jt-1} = k_{jt-1}$	$\bar{r}_{jt-1} > k_{jt-1}$
$z_{jt} = \bar{r}_{jt}/k_{jt}$	Positive	Positive	Positive
r_{jt}	Positive	Nil	Negative
Overall Systematic Risk	Positive	Positive	Uncertain

mon equity is equal to the capitalization rate at the start of the holding period and the fourth column summarizes the result when the condition in column two is reversed.

Although we have indicated that the effect of corporate growth on overall systematic risk is uncertain when $\bar{r}_{jt-1} > k_{jt-1}$, we feel that the case for hypothesizing that the relationship is usually a positive one is quite strong. Any tendency toward a negative relationship between growth and risk stemming from current, short-lived fluctuations in profits is almost certainly overcome by the positive relationship between growth and the risk stemming from changes in long run profitability which, by its long-run nature, is much larger in magnitude for most firms. Empirical evidence to support or reject this principal hypothesis will be presented in the chapters which follow.

Chapter VI

Empirical Review

I. INTRODUCTION

Since 1969 when Ball and Brown.[1] and Beaver et al.,[2] published their seminal works, in which they presented evidence of correlation between estimates of common stock risk and measures of the systematic variability of accounting income numbers, there have been a number of additional studies reported which employed various techniques in similar pursuits. The objectives of these studies have usually been stated to include one or more of the following:

(a) To test the usefulness of reported accounting numbers for purposes of assessing or predicting investment risk;

(b) To seek out new and more useful accounting numbers;

(c) To measure the association between common stock risk and corporate characteristics in such areas as dividend payout, growth, operating leverage, financial leverage, liquidity, profit margin, asset turnover, return on assets, return on equity, size, earnings variability, earnings growth variability, capitalization factor risk, published quality ratings, trading volume, share price, and exchange listing;

(d) To test hypotheses concerning the determinants of systematic stock risk; and

(e) In one case,[3] to measure the cost of capital for a particular activity in an industry where more than one major type of activity is undertaken by the firms making up the industry.

In view of the measurement techniques developed, the discussion of hypotheses concerning whether correlations are causal or spurious, and the opportunity to achieve an overview of the empirical outcomes of such studies, it may be useful to review some of the pertinent results. Section II reviews several of the studies most relevant to our work and Section III provides a summary and conclusion.

II. REVIEW OF SOME EMPIRICAL STUDIES

(a) Ball and Brown.[4]

On the basis of earlier work regarding the efficiency of capital markets with respect to reported accounting income numbers, Ball and Brown hypothesize that changes in corporate earnings cause changes in firm value and that this will cause an association between the systematic variability of earnings and the systematic risk of common stocks. Using data from 261 firms for 21 years, they computed the following time series regressions for each company:

$$R_{jt} = a_j + \beta_j R_{mt} + \varepsilon_{jt} \qquad (6.1)$$

and

$$r_{jt} = a_j + b_j r_{It} + e_{jt} \qquad (6.2)$$

where
R_{jt} = the holding period return on stock j in period t;
R_{mt} = holding period return on a market index in period t,
r_{jt} = either the level or temporal first difference of an accounting income number, and
r_{ij} = either the level or temporal first difference of an accounting income number index, as appropriate.

Then the cross-section correlation was estimated between the

R^2's of (6.1) and (6.2) as a measure of the degree of association between the systematic variance of market returns and the systematic variance of accounting income numbers. The correlation was minimal where income levels were used in (6.2) but it was greatly increased by the use of first differences (0.47 using operating income differences, 0.39 using net income differences, and 0.42 using earnings per share differences). In addition, the correlation between the estimates for β_j in (6.1) and b_j in (6.2) was calculated but only after the regressions were rerun using income numbers deflated by share price. These correlations were even higher, especially where first differences were used. However, the effect of deflating by the share price ratio is uncertain and full of theoretical problems.

Under ideal circumstances of no growth, the earnings price ratio is equal to the discount rate for expected future dividends provided the earnings figure used is *expected* future earnings and not realized earnings. The use of realized earnings adds information concerning systematic variability of earnings and the result can be thought of as a hybrid variable. The coefficient estimate is a combined estimate of the systematic variability of both the capitalization rate and earnings. However, all stocks have some growth rate (usually positive, but sometimes negative) for expected dividends and in that case equation (2.21) indicates that the earnings-price ratio may be written as

$$\frac{E(Y_{t+1})}{P_t} = \frac{k_t - a\bar{r}_t}{1 - a}, a < 1, k_t > a\bar{r}_t, \qquad (6.3)$$

where

$E(Y_{t+1})$ = expected earnings per share in period $t + 1$,
P_t = share price at the end of period t,
k_t = the capitalization rate,
a   = the rate of investment of equity as a fraction of earnings, and
$\bar{r}_t$ = the expected future return on net worth.

Thus, even if *expected* earnings per share were used in the earnings price ratio, the ratio is still a hybrid reflecting the capitalization rate, the expected rate of equity investment, and the expected return on net worth in future periods. Deflating realized earnings by share price makes the variable partly a capitalization variable, partly an earnings variable, partly a growth expectations variable and partly a profitability expectations variable. Introducing this variable and an index variable like it into a regression such as (6.2) means that the slope coefficient is a mixed estimate of the systematic variability of all of these factors. Consequently it contains much more information than a pure accounting income number variable, and indeed the results by Ball and Brown support this theoretical evidence.

(b) Beaver, Kettler and Scholes. [5]

In a study that was apparently independent of the previous work of Ball and Brown, these authors advanced this type of research by introducing additional corporate variables to explain estimates of systematic risk, by splitting their data into two intervals for purposes of inferring the stability of the variables and their contemporaneous correlations, by introducing a test of the usefulness of accounting variables as instruments for reducing the measurement error in systematic risk estimates for predicting future risk, and by attempting to reduce the effects of error in accounting variables by forming portfolios on the basis of the original and corrected systematic risk estimates.

The variables used by Beaver, Kettler and Scholes for each firm were:

(i) Market beta—the estimate of systematic risk computed using natural logarithms of monthly stock return relatives;

(ii) Average dividend payout—the ratio of the sum of dividends paid to the sum of earnings over the period concerned;

(iii) Average asset growth—the logarithm of initial over ending total assets in each period;

(iv) Average leverage—the average of total senior securities divided by total assets;

(v) Average asset size—the average of the logarithm of total assets;

(vi) Average liquidity—the average current ratio;

(vii) Earnings variability—the standard deviation of earnings deflated by lagged share price;

(viii) Accounting beta—the slope coefficient of the time series regression of earnings deflated by lagged share price for each firm on an index composed of the average of the same variable over all 307 firms in the sample.

Before reporting on their empirical work they discussed the basis for including each variable as a surrogate for the systematic risk of common stock. Some of their points are of particular interest in formulating our test design:

(i) *Dividend payout.* The authors observed that a low dividend payout rate may be associated with risky firms due to the reluctance of managements to undertake any unnecessary risk of having to cut dividends during a period of temporarily low earnings. To the extent that retention of earnings is associated with corporate growth this reasoning also indicates a spurious correlation between systematic risk and growth.

(ii) *Growth.* There are three additional reasons offered why growth may be spuriously correlated with systematic risk. First, growth is associated with excessive earnings opportunities which may attract competitive entry and contribute to corporate risk. Second, rapid growth may involve a greater than usual proportion of assets in new investments which may be risky. Third, risky firms may have rapid *ex post* growth due to a run of abnormally large transitory earnings components.

We tend to reject these last reasons for spurious correlation as not valid, although we agree with their opinion on dividend payout. First, there is no reason to believe that competitive entry is a *systematic* source of risk. In fact, it may be a source of valuable negative correlation if competitive entry tends to occur during periods of booming capital markets and economies. The risk of competitive entry or even market share disputes is probably highly diversifiable from the investor point of view and should not show up as an important determinant of systematic risk. Second, as the authors point out, it is not immediately obvious that new corporate investments are more risky than seasoned investments and we would add that it is even less obvious that they have greater *systematic* risk. Third, as the authors also point out, risky firms may have greater probability of a run of abnormally large transitory earnings components which give rise to rapid *ex post* growth but the same is also true of a run of abnormally small transitory earnings components which would give rise to low or negative growth. Therefore, this is not a source of correlation of growth and systematic risk.

(iii) *Leverage.* It can be easily shown that, as leverage is added, the return on net worth becomes more volatile as a residual number. Thus leverage appears to be a causal source of systematic risk. However, there is an offsetting effect of leverage on holding-period returns on stocks. As the fixed payment obligations of a firm increase relative to income, a rise in the general structure of interest rates will have a less damaging effect on the firm's residual value, as the owners of the fixed liability securities will tend to absorb a greater amount of the capital loss. This effect is particularly significant when interest rates fluctuate by large amounts as in the last decade. Therefore, the sign of the correlation between leverage and systematic risk is uncertain, especially in recent years.

(iv) *Liquidity.* The authors posit that liquidity will not be strongly associated with systematic risk since the differential effect of varying proportions of current assets to total assets will be small relative to the differential risk of noncurrent assets between firms. We tend to agree with this although there may be additional factors at work. Increased liquidity may tend to allow a firm more flexibility in the event of sudden changes in the firm's environment. Thus one could argue that liquidity will be negatively associated with systematic risk. However, it may also be true that liquidity acts as an inverse proxy for earnings variability since firms with volatile earnings will tend to keep a higher liquidity ratio for purposes of financial safety and because volatile inventory demands require higher inventory levels. In summary, the sign of the correlation between liquidity and systematic risk is uncertain.

(v) *Asset size.* Although larger firms tend to have a lower relative dispersion of earnings and a lower rate of default because of greater diversification of investments, on average, the authors correctly note that this diversification should not result in lower systematic risk which, by definition, is not diversifiable. It is not clear why size enters as an explanatory variable in the study.

(vi) *Variability of earnings-price ratios.* This variable was included because it performed better than accounting income numbers deflated by net worth and total assets in a pilot study.

(vii) *Covariability in earnings-price ratios.* The reason for including a measure of systematic variability of earnings is self explanatory but our preceding criticism of the use of share price as a deflator by Ball and Brown applies here as well.

The empirical results reported by Beaver, Kettler and Scholes were based on two levels of aggregation. Each test was run using single firm observations which is the lowest level of aggregation. Then the firms were grouped into portfolios of five firms each according to the size of their estimates for systematic stock risk. The means of the grouped observations were used to obtain the results reported at this level of aggregation.

A number of comments are appropriate here with respect to this grouping based on Johnston's treatment of the technique from an econometric viewpoint.[6] He shows that forming groups of equal numbers of observations retains homoscedasticity if the original data has that desirable property. Thus ordinary least squares is just as applicable to the grouped data as to the original observations. However, that is where the similarity ceases. First, the sampling variances of regression coefficients from grouped data are greater and are minimized only by grouping on a variable which will maximize the *between* group variation of the *independent* variable in relation to the *within* group variation. However, Beaver, Kettler and Scholes grouped the data on the basis of the estimates of systematic market risk which is full of measurement error and is usually considered as the *dependent* variable in work of this kind. Hence we can expect a substantial loss in efficiency under this grouping method. It might be noted that grouping on an accounting risk measure would be little better, although the drop in efficiency wouldn't be as great, since that method would exacerbate the bias due to errors in the independent variable. Moreover,

Johnston cites a study by Haitovsky in which the coefficient signs, magnitudes and standard error estimates are highly unstable with respect to the method of aggregation and the particular independent variable used for the grouping when more than one independent variable is available from which to choose.[7] In addition, grouping causes substantial increases in R^2's (and correlation coefficients). The information this provides with respect to the original observations is ambiguous and may be misleading.

With respect to loss of efficiency from grouping, Johnston cites a simulation study by Orcutt et al., in which they find that the dispersion of sampling distributions of regression coefficients increases with the degree of aggregation and the rate of increase is greater than expected from the simple reduction in degrees of freedom.[8] This is possible due to the increased correlation among variables in the grouped data which results in increased sampling variances for coefficients. They also found a tendency for these sampling variances to be underestimated. Johnston shows that R^2's tend to be misleading in grouped data and also cites a paper by Cramer[9] in which he shows that correlation coefficients also increase when observations are grouped. In summary, to paraphrase Johnston, grouping observations appears to be a misguided practice.

For each firm in each period 1947–1956 and 1957–1965 inclusive, Beaver et al. calculated the variables previously described. They then estimated the between-period correlation coefficient for each variable. While both rank-order correlations and product-moment correlations were computed we have reproduced only the latter coefficient estimates in Table 6.1 below, as reported in the original source.

The authors reported the contemporaneous correlation between the estimates of systematic stock risk and the other variables. The product-moment correlations reported are reproduced in Table 6.2 for both individual firm observations and five-firm portfolios grouped on estimated systematic risk.

In general the results speak for themselves. Portfolio means for the variables are more highly correlated with the corresponding estimates of systematic stock risk as Johnston indicates will be

Table 6.1. Between Period Product-Moment Correlations from Individual Firm Data

Variable	Correlation Coefficient
Systematic stock risk estimates	.594*
Average dividend payout rate	.429
Growth of total assets	.205
Average leverage (book values)	.768
Average liquidity	.883
Average asset size	.963
Standard deviation of earnings/lagged price	.410
Accounting beta for earnings/lagged price	− .060

* With 307 observations coefficients with an absolute value greater than .094 are "significant" at the 5 percent probability level in a one-tail test.

the case, although the meaning of this is ambiguous with respect to the original data. The average dividend payout rate is very negatively correlated with systematic risk as expected from either the authors' hypothesis that risky firms have low payout rate policies, our hypothesis that systematic risk is a positive causal function of corporate growth, or the well-known Gordon hypothesis that stock risk is a positive function of the earnings retention rate.[10] Our growth hypothesis can explain the result

Table 6.2. Contemporaneous Product-Moment Correlation Between Estimates of Stock Risk and Other Risk Measures

| Variable | Correlation Coefficient | | | |
| | 1947–1956 | | 1957–1965 | |
	Firms	Portfolios	Firms	Portfolios
Average dividend payout rate	− .50*	− .77**	− .24*	− .45**
Growth of total assets	.23	.51	.03	.07
Average leverage (book values)	.23	.45	.25	.56
Average liquidity	− .13	− .44	− .01	− .01
Average asset size	− .07	− .13	− .16	− .30
$\hat{\sigma}$ (earnings/lagged price)	.58	.77	.36	.62
Accounting beta (earnings/ lagged price)	.39	.67	.23	.46

*5 percent "significance" level is ± 0.094, N = 307.
**5 percent "significance" level is ± 0.211, N = 61.

provided only that dividend policy is a better proxy for expected growth than the past rate of growth of total assets which may well be the case. Average leverage appears with a positive correlation as predicted while average liquidity has a negative correlation for 1947–1956 and is neutral for 1957–1965. Size appears with a "significant" negative sign in the second period only and the last two variables appear as expected.

In testing the usefulness of "accounting" numbers as instruments for removing measurement error from first-period estimates of systematic risk in order to forecast second-period risk, the authors found that dividend payout, growth of assets and earnings/lagged price variability served best and the "corrected" estimates explained 24 percent of the variance in second-period estimates vs. 21 percent explained by the "uncorrected" values for individual securities. The corresponding R^2,s for the portfolios were 37 percent and 63 percent, respectively, with portfolios formed by ranking on the "corrected" first period estimates. Once again, these last figures are misleading in terms of the individual firm data.

(c) Pettit and Westerfield.[11]

This study appears to be one of the best efforts so far in the development of a theory relating systematic variability of earnings and capitalization rates to estimates of systematic risk. The chief drawback of the study is the failure of the authors to consider corporate growth in their theoretical model.

Briefly, if cash income is expected to be C^* in every future period and r is the capitalization rate, the value of a stock is given by

$$P = \frac{C^*}{r}. \tag{6.4}$$

For a small change in C^* or r the realized return on the stock after the change is

$$R' = \frac{dP + C_i^*}{P} \tag{6.5}$$

where C_i^* is the cash received (assumed equal to the expected receipt) and dP is the change in price due to a change in C* or r. However,

$$dP = \frac{dC^*}{r} - \frac{dr}{r^2} \tag{6.6}$$

and

$$R' = \frac{dC^*}{C^*} - \frac{dr}{r} + r \tag{6.7}$$

If this holds for both the jth stock and the market portfolio of stocks the systematic risk of the jth stock will have two factors which the authors call the cash flow factor and the capitalization factor. In particular, the systematic risk or market beta of stock j will be given by

$$\beta'_j = \gamma \beta_{cj} + (1 - \gamma)\beta_{rj} \tag{6.8}$$

where

β_{cj} = the jth firm's cash flow beta,
β_{rj} = the jth firm's capitalization beta, and
$$\gamma_j = \frac{\text{Var}(dC_m^*/C_m^*)}{\text{Var}(dC_m^*/C_m^*) + \text{Var}(dr_m/r_m)}.$$

The empirical work by Pettit and Westerfield was conducted for purposes of testing this result. Unfortunately, the model assumptions are overly restrictive in three aspects. First, there is no provision for growth. Second, investors are assumed to receive expected cash flows in every holding period. Third, changes in the expected cash flow or the capitalization rate are restricted to infinitesimal amounts by the use of derivatives to model the movements. These assumptions limit the insights available from the analysis to a considerable extent.

Using data for 338 firms for the period 1947–1956 and 543 firms for 1957–1968 the authors computed the following variables for each:

(i) *Market beta.* This was estimated for each firm in each period by regressing at least 60 monthly holding-period returns on an appropriate market index relative.

   (ii) *Cash flow beta.* First an earnings index was computed for each firm in each period by dividing annual earnings by the firm's average earnings. Next, this index for each firm was regressed on time. Third, the residuals from this regression for each firm were regressed on a similarly constructed series from the quarterly earnings per share of the Standard and Poor Composite Index. The resulting slope coefficient is the cash flow beta for each firm with the effects of size and growth eliminated.

  (iii) *Capitalization rate beta.* The slope coefficient of a regression of the percentage change in the earnings-price ratio for a firm on the earnings price ratio of Standard and Poor's Composite Price Index. Note that our previous comments on the use of this variable by Ball and Brown also apply here. In particular, the variable is a complex mixture of the systematic variability of the capitalization rate, the expected rate of equity investment, and the expected rate of return on net worth. It is not, therefore, a pure capitalization rate beta.

  (iv) *Dividend payout.* The sum of dividends divided by the sum of earnings in each period.

   (v) *Leverage.* The book value of total liabilities and preferred stock divided by the average market value of equity each period.

  (vi) *Firm size.* The average total assets each period.

 (vii) *Liquidity.* The average current ratio each period.

(viii) *Growth.* The slope coefficient of the regression of the earnings per share index described in (ii) on time.

Using these estimates, the between-period correlations were estimated for each variable as were the contemporaneous correlations between variables. In addition, the same correlations were computed using portfolios of 5 and 20 firms formed by grouping on the estimated market betas. The comments applicable to the use of this technique by Beaver, Kettler and Scholes also apply here. Rather than reproduce all of these results here, we will only comment that for the individual firm data the market beta correlations with the cash flow betas, the capitalization rate betas, the dividend payout ratios, and the growth rate of earnings per share were about .3, .2, − .4, and .2, respectively. In addition the cross-section correlation of dividend payout with earnings growth was − .254 for 1947 − 1956 and − .434 for 1956 − 1965.

In order to test the hypothesis that market betas were equal to the convex combination of a cash flow beta and a capitalization rate beta as reviewed earlier, the market betas for each period were regressed on the variables described using individual firm data and portfolios of five and twenty firms. The results reported for the individual firm data are summarized in Table 6.3.

The first thing to note concerning these results is that the coefficients on $\hat{\beta}'_i$ fall far short of their theoretical value of 1.0 and the intercepts are much larger than zero. This may be due in part to errors in $\hat{\beta}'_i$ which would bias its coefficients downward and the intercept upward, and the coefficients reported using portfolios grouped on the market betas tend to improve toward their theoretical magnitudes. However, given the problems of aggregating data on the dependent variable the conclusion to draw from this is ambiguous.

The second comment to make is that the $\hat{\beta}'_i$ variable alone gives a

Table 6.3. Regression of Market Beta vs. Contemporaneous Variables

Variable	1947–1956 Regressions			1957–1968 Regressions		
	(a)	(b)	(c)	(d)	(e)	(f)
Constant	.947	1.417	1.596	.892	1.215	1.257
$\hat{\beta}'_i = \gamma\hat{\beta}_{ci} + (1-\gamma)\hat{\beta}_{ri}$	.064	.052		.118	.108	
	(4.74)	(4.54)		(7.05)	(6.98)	
Dividend Payout Ratio		− 1.000	− 1.159		− .671	− .285
		(− .845)	(− 9.32)		(− 9.69)	(− 7.65)
Growth of Earnings		.555	.389		.133	.398
		(3.08)	(2.16)		(.76)	(2.20)
Leverage			− .037			.012
			(− 1.96)			(.78)
Size			− .020			− .030
			(− .89)			(− 3.66)
Adjusted R²	.057	.275	.240	.080	.260	.176
N	338	338	338	534	534	534

very low R^2 value which increases markedly when the dividend payout and earnings growth variables are added. Again, this may be due to error in $\hat{\beta}'_i$ but it is more likely due to market beta also being a function of dividend policy and/or growth, as our theoretical results suggest. Growth and dividend payout have correlation coefficients of approximately -0.4 as we noted earlier and this appears to be a sufficiently large absolute magnitude for them to act as close substitutes as indicated by their alternating contributions in regressions (b) and (e). Moreover, given that $\hat{\beta}'_i$ contains a measure of the systematic variability of earnings, the spurious negative correlation between dividend payout and systematic risk hypothesized by Beaver, Kettler and Scholes should not appear as strongly in regressions (b) and (e) as in regressions (c) and (d) if it does exist in fact. That appears to be the case for regressions (b) and (c) with the coefficient on the dividend payout increasing in negative magnitude and "significance" when $\hat{\beta}'_i$ is removed. However, the opposite is true comparing regressions (e) and (f). Therefore it is difficult to reach any strong conclusion concerning the relationship of dividend policy to earnings variability and systematic risk.

Leverage enters with mixed sign indicating its relative overall unimportance as a risk determinant and size appears to have a small negative effect which is not consistently "significant."

(d) Gordon.[12]

As part of a much larger study of the cost of capital for public utilities Gordon conducted an empirical study of the relationship between market betas and variables which he has frequently hypothesized as important in stock valuation and the cost of equity capital. These include the return on common equity, the earnings-retention rate, the stock-financing rate (defined as a fraction of net worth), the book value of leverage, and two variables specific to utility data: the percentage of sales which are electricity sales, and an index of the quality of earnings. The return on common equity, which was not considered in the studies reviewed above, was included on the basis of what might be termed a commensurate

rate of return hypothesis with regard to net worth. That is, Gordon offers the hypothesis that growth variables are a function of the rate of return expected on net worth, and the rate of return on net worth will tend toward a general equilibrium return that is commensurate with the risk involved. The relationship is clear for utilities since the regulators attempt to set allowed rates with the risk in mind. However, for nonregulated firms the relationship must rely upon the competitive entry and exit of firms to establish commensurate returns for any given industry. This may be more or less certain than the utility case but it is nevertheless apt to cause a spurious relationship between growth and systematic risk.

Gordon ran a regression of market beta estimates on the above-mentioned variables for each year, 1958 to 1968, using data from his sample of 54 electric utilities. In general, the coefficients were positive and significant for the return on common equity, the retention rate, and the stock financing rate. The other variables performed very inconsistently and were not often "significant" at a 5 percent level of probability.

(e) Logue and Merville.[13]

The most interesting aspect of this empirical study relating market beta estimates to underlying explanatory variables is their hypothesis that profitability may be inversely correlated with systematic risk since highly profitable firms are less prone to failure. They may also be those firms which enjoy permanent barriers to entry which allow greater product price discretion. However, they also note that the correlation between profitability and risk may be of the opposite sign, since more profitable firms can employ greater leverage without risk of default. This effect tends to be mitigated, however, by the uncertain relationship that is found between leverage and estimates of systematic risk. These hypotheses together with Gordon's, mentioned above, indicate that the sign of the correlation between profitability and market beta estimates may be unpredictable and possibly unstable as conditions of the business cycle change.

Using data for 287 firms from the Fortune 500 for 1966 to 1970, the authors estimated a regression of market beta estimates on corporate averages for the current ratio, short-term liabilities over total assets, long-term debt over total assets, the dividend payout ratio, growth of total assets, asset turnover, profit margin, and the logarithm of total assets. With an R^2 of 0.25 the coefficients for both leverage variables were "significantly" positive at the 5 percent probability level while the coefficients for profit margin and logarithm of total assets were "significantly" negative. The separate hypotheses that coefficients for the current ratio, dividend payout, growth of total assets and turnover were equal to zero could not be rejected at the 5 percent probability level. The same regression, using return on assets instead of turnover and profit margin separately, conserved the results for other variables and gave a "significant" negative coefficient for the profitability variable. Thus Gordon's finding of a positive coefficient for a profitability variable using utilities is contradicted using data for industrials.

(f) Gordon and Halpern.[14]

An interesting study by these authors for the purpose of estimating the cost of capital to the airline industry for carrying mail has produced the result that market beta estimates are highly correlated with systematic variability estimates for annual *ex post* growth rates in earnings calculated using overlapping quarterly data to obtain four annual observations for each firm each year. In developing their methodology the authors show that if expected corporate growth is nil, if investors believe that most recent earnings are an unbiased estimate of all future earnings, if the capitalization rate for expected dividends is constant over time, and if the interest bill doesn't change, then the holding period rate of return on a stock is given by

$$R'_t = \frac{D_t + P_t - P_{t-1}}{P_{t-1}}$$

$$= \frac{(X_t - iB)(1-\tau) + (X_t - iB)(1-\tau)/k - (X_{t-1} - iB)(1-\tau)/k}{(X_{t-1} - iB)(1-\tau)/k}$$

$$= \frac{(X_t - iB)k + (X_t - X_{t-1})}{X_{t-1} - iB} \tag{6.9}$$

where

X_t = earnings before interest and taxes in period t,

τ = corporate tax rate,

iB = interest on long-term debt during period t, and

k = the dividend capitalization rate.

Alternatively, the authors could have written

$$R'_t = \frac{(X_t - iB)(1 + k)}{(X_{t-1} - iB)} - 1. \tag{6.10}$$

Since the *ex post* growth of earnings is equal to

$$g'_t = \frac{(X_t - iB)}{X_{t-1} - iB} - 1 \tag{6.11}$$

it follows that R'_t and g'_t are *perfectly* correlated provided the model assumptions hold. When X_t is the only random variable generating uncertainty in R'_t and g'_t their correlation coefficient is

$$\rho = \frac{\text{Cov}\left[\dfrac{X_t - iB}{X_{t-1} - iB} - 1, \dfrac{(X_t - iB)(1 + k)}{X_{t-1} - iB} - 1\right]}{\left[\text{Var}\left[\dfrac{X_t - iB}{X_{t-1} - iB} - 1\right]\right]^{1/2}\left[\text{Var}\left[\dfrac{(X_t - iB)(1 + k)}{X_{t-1} - iB} - 1\right]\right]^{1/2}} \tag{6.12}$$

$$= 1.$$

If the assumptions hold it is also true that the *systematic variability* of *ex post* growth is equal to the systematic variability of the *ex post* return on the stock.

However, we would comment as follows: Under the assumptions of the model it is also true that earnings or earnings deflated by net worth are perfectly correlated with R'_t and the systematic variability of earnings or return on net worth is equal to the systematic variability of *ex post* market returns. Thus it is not the theoretical model showing that *ex post* earnings growth is closely related to holding period returns under restrictive assumptions that makes growth such a good variable. The same conclusion would have been drawn had the authors compared the stock return with earnings, say. What makes earnings growth a good variable is an econometric property of the data, in particular a strong positive association between the systematic variability of *ex post* earnings growth and the expected growth of earnings in the future. This would make the systematic variability of *ex post* earnings growth an excellent explanatory variable for systematic risk since it would proxy for both the systematic variability of earnings and for expected corporate growth, which our analysis indicates is a causal variable in determining systematic risk. In addition, there are two other factors which would make the variable used a very good one. First, systematic variability in *ex post* growth in earnings per share contains information concerning variability in earnings retention rates which may affect share values. Second, the authors used the logarithm of earnings relatives in implementing the tests which is very much like using deflated first differences. If the earnings index has high autocorrelation ($\rho > .5$) the use of first differences is a superior regression technique in terms of efficiency in estimating the coefficients.[15] In any case, the use of systematic variability in *ex post* earnings growth was a useful variable for the purposes of the study. Using data for 49 firms with four overlapping observations on growth each year for 1957–1968, the correlation between the market beta, which was estimated from logarithms of monthly returns, and systematic growth variability was 0.66. The 5 percent significance level for 49 observations is 0.24.

(g) Other Studies.

Studies other than those mentioned above are basically of two types. Those by Gonedes,[16] and Beaver and Manegold[17] are additional efforts to determine the best way to specify income numbers in estimating their systematic variability with an income number index. Beaver and Manegold try several methods and their results show that there is little to choose from between ordinary least squares estimates using return on net worth, which is the simplest, and more complicated techniques using first differences and similar two-step procedures based on the autoregression coefficient followed by an heuristic bayesian adjustment. The studies by Rosenberg and McKibben, Breen and Lerner, and Melicher provide additional evidence of the value of underlying variables as proxies for systematic risk.[18]

III. SUMMARY AND CONCLUSIONS

The literature which we have reviewed in the foregoing section has presented a number of soundly based hypotheses and empirical evidence concerning the associations to be found between estimates of the systematic risk of common stocks and a number of so-called accounting number based variables that appear to perform, with varying degrees of consistency, as proxies for risk.

With regard to income number based proxies, a number of authors found that standardized estimates of the covariance of income levels or first differences, deflated by a market or book value size variable, with a similarly constructed index for many firms performed consistently in explaining a "significant" amount of variation in estimates of market betas for stocks, However, we observed that the use of market value variables such as lagged share price transform these income number based variables into complex hybrids that contain information on the systematic covariability of other factors, such as the capitalization rate, the expected rate of investment, and the expected value of return on net worth for the future. In another case, the use of an estimate of the covariability of *ex post* earnings growth with a similar widely based index resulted in a proxy that perhaps included information on the expected rate of growth of future earnings. While this variable was suitable for the particular study in which it was employed we would be incorrect in using it as an estimate of earnings risk in our tests of the hypothesis that stock risk is a positive function of expected growth. The variable might proxy for expected growth causing our explicit growth variable to perform ambiguously. We also observed in a recent study that there is little to choose from between straightforward estimates of the covariability of return on net worth with a similar index and more complex estimates using heuristic bayesian corrections of coefficients estimated with two-step econometric procedures designed to deal with any serial correlation that might exist in corporate earnings. Our conclusion with respect to an appropriate estimator for earnings risk is that a regression of the rate of return on net worth against an index of the same variable for a large number of firms is about as satisfactory an estimator as one can achieve, with the possible exception of such an estimator with measurement error removed by the use of instrumental variables.

All of the studies which incorporated one or more estimates of corporate growth; such as the dividend payout rate (a negative proxy for expected growth), the average growth of earnings or assets, the retention ratio multiplied by average return on net worth, or the average stock financing rate multiplied by average return on net worth; found those estimates to have a large amount of explanatory power for systematic risk estimates relative to the estimates of systematic variability of earnings. However, there are possible explanations for this even if systematic risk is not a causal function of growth. Of the reasons put forth by various authors we find three to be quite plausible. First, as Gordon has long contended, share risk may be a causal function of earnings retention (or dividend policy) per se. If this is so, the positive correlation between retention of earnings and the rate of corporate growth may give rise to other estimates of corporate growth acting as proxies for retention policy. Second, dividend payout may be a negative function of the variability of earnings according to the hypothesis that managers seek to avoid dividend cuts during periods of low earnings. Again, since dividend payout and corporate growth are inversely correlated this may result in a positive spurious correlation between growth and systematic risk. Third, the rate of return on real investment in a given industry may approach a general equilibrium rate which is determined in part by the degree of risk in the industry. Since the rate of growth of a company may be partly a function of the level of earnings it is possible that the general equilibrium relationship between risk and return may result in a spurious correlation between growth and systematic risk. A fourth, and in our opinion less plausible or at least less important source of spurious correlation, is the hypothesis that high returns which are incentives to growth also attract competitive entry which is a source of risk. That this is an important source of systematic risk is doubtful for two reasons. First, competitive entry may not be a cause of *systematic* risk and second, many instances can be found where high returns are present because of effective barriers to entry which reduce competition to a great degree and provide a great deal of stability to industry earnings. In any case, in view of the plausibility of the existence of three sources of spurious association between growth and risk and the possible existence of a fourth, any test of our causal growth-risk hypothesis will need to have the capacity to remove these effects in order for the test to be useful as evidence one way or the other.

In addition to systematic earnings variability, dividend policy, and growth, the studies we reviewed contained evidence on the contributions of corporate leverage, liquidity, size, and profitability to systematic risk. Leverage is an important variable in the extant theory of finance but it performs very inconsistently in explaining systematic risk differences across firms. Nevertheless, its theoretical importance assures it a role in any study of the determinants of risk. Not so for liquidity and size. Although liquidity is an intuitively attractive variable as a determinant of risk, it is short on justification in a formal sense. Moreover, liquidity is apt to be strongly correlated with earnings variability for the spurious reason that managers of risky firms follow the sound practice of maintaining high current ratios as safety factors. Hence, the inclusion of liquidity as an intuitively attractive causal variable would, in all likelihood, result in the estimation of a spurious relationship with possibly serious misspecification problems as a result. Size has even weaker justification for inclusion at the theoretical level. Systematic risk, by definition, is undiversifiable risk and thus the increased diversification of real investments by large firms should not result in lower systematic risk. The negative relationships noted between estimates of systematic risk and size may be due to the positive correlation of market betas with total variability of corporate returns and the negative correlation of size with these returns. The problem is one of an econometric nature and is best solved by excluding size as a variable.

The inclusion of profitability as an explanatory variable has several aspects to consider. As noted above, the return on net worth may be causally related to the risk of the investments. Riskier investments require larger expected returns in general equilibrium. Thus return on net worth has a theoretical place in an association with systematic risk of positive sign. However, as one study observed, firms with high profitability may have low risk because profitable firms have a smaller probability of failure during declines in economic activity. We have also noted that profitable firms may also tend to be those which enjoy stability as a result of barriers to entry. Thus profitability may be negatively correlated with systematic risk. A third aspect is that profitability is associated with growth and thus it may act as its proxy to some extent. Therefore the sign is uncertain, a priori, and, in addition, we should be cautious in interpreting a test of our causal growth-risk hypothesis in its presence.

A Test of the Effect of Corporate Growth on Systematic Market Risk: Canadian Data

I. INTRODUCTION

In the previous chapters we have developed a theoretical basis for the hypothesis that systematic stock risk is a positive function of the growth rate of expected total corporate earnings and dividends. The purpose of this chapter and the one following is to test that hypothesis with Canadian and U.S. data. In this chapter, Section II deals with the test design in light of our review of previous empirical work and theoretical considerations. Section III describes the Canadian data employed and measurement of the variables concerned. The empirical results are presented in Section IV. Section V provides a summary. In the following chapter we report on further empirical tests with U.S. data.

II. TEST DESIGN

The most important empirically testable implication of the theoretical analysis reported in previous chapters is that the risk to a diversified investor of holding a particular common stock is, among other things, a positive function of the rate at which the

101

market expects the firm's total earnings and dividends to grow in the future. As discussed in our review of the literature in the preceding chapter, however, there are a number of other factors which determine stock risk besides expected growth, and our empirical design must take these factors into consideration in order to avoid confounding results. Moreover, the risk of doing business in a particular industry or product area may cause managerial decisions that effect the rate of corporate growth, either directly or through an underlying variable which has some effect on growth. It will therefore be necessary to hold such factors constant in order to actually test our hypothesis that expected growth is a causal variable in determining stock risk. The following subsections are devoted to a discussion of the potential sources of confusion and the variables which are necessary to avoid potentially confounding results in a cross-section regression aimed at testing our main hypothesis.

Undiversifiable Earnings Variability

In a cross-section regression of market betas on estimates of corporate growth expectations it is important to include a variable which measures the different levels of undiversifiable business risk which firms in the sample must face. As our review of the literature has shown, a standardized measure of the covariance of a firm's earnings with a widely based index of corporate earnings (i.e., an earnings beta) is capable of explaining at least a small part of the variance in estimates of market betas. Therefore, inclusion of an earnings beta is advisable since it will reduce the unexplained variance in the dependent variable. In addition, omitting a measure of business risk would leave open the possibility that the growth variable would proxy for business risk. As we discussed in the literature review, corporate growth may be positively associated with business risk for several reasons. First, riskier lines of business offer greater expected profits in general equilibrium and greater expected profits may contribute to greater growth as indicated by the product $a\bar{r}_t$. Second, managers of riskier firms may retain a greater fraction of profits for reasons of corporate safety and because of an aversion to cutting dividends. This may cause a greater rate of total equity investment because of greater equity capital availability, although the tendency for riskier firms to retain a greater fraction of their earnings would be at least partly offset by a reduced stock issue rate or a higher rate of share repurchase. In any case, it is probable that firms with greater business risk will have higher growth of expected earnings and dividends. Therefore, a measure of business risk is required in the regression to avoid a potential bias in the coefficient on the growth variable.

Retention Proportion of Equity Financing

From our review of the controversy over the valuation effects of dividend policy we concluded that the effect of dividend policy on stock risk has not been completely resolved. Our analysis supports the conclusion that dividend policy, per se, has no effect on stock risk in perfectly competitive capital markets. However, it is a fact that transaction costs and different taxation rates for capital gians vs. dividends make capital markets less than perfect, to say nothing of the imperfect and costly nature of information flow which makes dividend policy a source of information to investors. Thus, it is conceivable that dividend policy could be a factor in determining stock risk. Moreover, since managers of highly risky firms may pursue conservative dividend payout policies, it is wise to include a dividend or retention policy variable to prevent the growth variable from proxying for either a dividend policy effect, per se, or for business risk which may be correlated with earnings retention rates. The proportion of equity financing obtained from retention of earnings is a suitable variable since it reflects dividend policy, per se, and it will not act as a proxy for expected growth because it is independent of the equity financing rate. In addition to helping to avoid confounding investment policy with dividend policy, this variable should provide additional evidence on the dividend effect controversy.

Debt/Equity Ratio

Modigliani and Miller[1] and Hamada[2] have clearly demonstrated that the risk of common stock is a positive function of leverage in the sense that earnings are a residual and made more uncertain as leverage increases. On the other hand, Haugen and Wichern[3] have shown that stock risk may be reduced by leverage if the interest rate elasticity of the debt is sufficiently great to reduce the inverse relationship between capitalization rates and stock prices. Thus corporate leverage is theoretically justified as a variable for inclusion in the regression. Ideally, a measure of the interest rate elasticity of the debt should be included as well. However, existing sources of data do not provide adequate details of maturities, coupon rates, sinking funds and call provisions to make this feasible. In the absence of a duration statistic for each firm, the leverage variable will proxy for duration as well as leverage and its coefficient may have either a positive or negative partial correlation with market betas.

Return on Common Equity

As noted in the subsection above concerning undiversifiable earnings variability, return on common equity investment is jointly determined with business risk in general equilibrium. Firms require greater return expectations for investments with greater undiversifiable risk, so we expect returns in risky industries to be high. Similarly, returns on investment in a low risk industry are expected to be low, provided the industry is perfectly competitive. If the industry is not competitive, however, the returns may be relatively high because of effective barriers to entry that allow excessive returns and reduce risk simultaneously. Since expected growth is determined partly by profitability expectations, and profitability may be linked either positively or negatively with business risk, a profitability variable should be included although its partial correlation with market beta may be of either sign.

Liquidity

In our review of the literature in the previous chapter, we concluded that the relationship between corporate liquidity and stock risk is not clear. On one hand, illiquidity may cause a stock to be a risky investment. On the other hand, a situation of high business risk may cause managers to adopt a policy of high liquidity for safety reasons. Moreover, it is not clear that there is a predictable relationship between liquidity and corporate growth since firms tend to be most illiquid in situations of rapid growth, and in situations where growth prospects are dim. Since there is neither a predictable association between risk and liquidity or liquidity and growth, we have elected not to include liquidity as a variable in our regression estimates. To do so would mean running the risk of reducing the efficiency of the regression, with little, if any, theoretical justification for doing so.

Corporate Size

There appears to be little justification for including a corporate size variable in an empirical study of *systematic* risk. The systematic variability of earnings should be independent of size on theoretical grounds. Moreover, the theoretical relationship between size and expected future growth rates is not clear, although it is likely true that a few relatively small firms may have very large growth *rate* potentials. The absence of theoretical justification for including a size variable, together with the need to avoid inefficiency in estimation, is sufficient reason to omit it from the empirical tests.

Expected Growth

The main purpose is to test for a positive correlation between stock risk and expected growth of total earnings while holding other factors, such as business risk, dividend policy, and leverage, constant as discussed above. Consequently, proxies for the market expectation of future corporate growth will be used to test our hypothesis. A positive coefficient will indicate empirical support for our main hypothesis that expected corporate growth is a positive causal factor in determining common stock risk.

III. MEASUREMENT OF THE VARIABLES

The *dependent variable* in our hypothesis is the systematic risk (*market beta*) of the holding period return on stocks at the start of each holding period (4.22). It is the standardized covariance of the distribution of the holding period return on the jth stock with the distribution of the holding period return on the market portfolio. Given that we are unable to observe the joint *ex ante* distribution concerned each period, as perceived by investors according to capital asset pricing theory, the empirical method of estimating the parameter concerned for a given stock is to run a time series regression using historical holding period returns on the stock vs. those on an index of stocks. The result is a best linear unbiased estimate of each firm's systematic risk provided a number of conditions are true, including (a) serial independence in holding period returns, (b) cross-section independence in residual error, (c) independence of regressor and residual error, (d) stationary population parameters over time, and (e) finite holding-period return variances.

In addition, if holding-period returns are normally distributed, the resulting coefficient estimates will have normal distributions which will allow statistical inference on the basis of computed standard errors or "t" values of regression coefficients in the absence of heteroscedasticity in the residuals.

Whether or not the above conditions hold has frequently been the subject of study in the past. In general, stock returns and indexes have very low serial correlation and the cross section independence of residual errors holds well when a broadly based index is employed.[4] The same is true for independence of regressor and error. At the level of individual securities, Sharpe and Cooper have presented evidence in the form of probability transition matrices for market beta estimates that indicates systematic risk is unstable over time.[5] Blume has indicated that market betas tend to move toward an overall average of 1.0 as time passes.[6] Our own theoretical work indicates that systematic risk will change as underlying causal variables such as expected growth change. Gonedes has presented evidence that the loss of power of market beta estimates in predicting future estimates due to lack of stationarity as historical observations are added trades off evenly with the loss of prediction power due to increased measurement error as observations are removed when about seven years of monthly data are employed.[7]

If population parameters for systematic risk are unstable over time, there is little we can do but heed the evidence of Gonedes and use seven years of monthly observations. As to whether or not the variance of holding period returns are finite, there is some indication by Fama, who first raised the issue, that he believes the assumption of finite variances may be justified in the normal course of empirical work.[8] Moreover, we are unable to observe the *ex ante* distributions of holding period returns and it may be the case that variances are finite. The empirical support invoked for the finite variance hypothesis is also consistent with the hypothesis that returns are from Student t distributions.[9] Our procedure will be to report standard errors divided by the coefficient estimates which may be taken as t-statistics under the assumptions that variances are finite and distributions are symmetric stable. This amounts to the assumption that returns are normally distributed.

In using historical returns for estimating market betas, it is a frequent practice to use the natural logarithm of the holding-period-return relative rather than the return relative itself, for two reasons. One is that the continuously compounded return which is obtained from the transformation is thought to be fitted better by the normal distribution since holding-period-return relatives are truncated from below at zero. Secondly, in the absence of a consensus on the appropriate holding period for investors, it is convenient to use the continuously compounded return since the systematic risk parameter thus estimated is invariant to the holding period assumed. However, these problems would seem to be dominated by an even greater theoretical issue which arises when the logarithm transformation is used. Consider the frequently studied case where utility of holding-period returns is assumed to be well represented by the logarithm function. This function is particularly attractive since it possesses the intuitively appealing attribute of constant relative risk aversion. It seems clear that investors with logarithmic utility functions will have as their objective the maximization of the expected value of the logarithm of holding-period-return relatives and will ignore the variance if their goal is to maximize expected utility. Accordingly, the systematic covariability of the logarithm of holding-period returns will not be of concern to investors, not will its underlying determinants such as growth be of any consequence.

In order to avoid the possibility of our estimate of systematic risk having no relevance, we prefer to base the estimate on the holding-period-return relative itself and tolerate the fact that the resulting dependent variable may be from a distribution more closely resembled by the lognormal than the normal. In addition, we will need to assume that the relevant holding period for investors is one month in order to employ monthly historical returns over seven-year intervals. This is recommended by Gonedes' results and is also ideally suited to the data available.[10]

Accordingly, market beta estimates were computed for each of 65 Canadian Companies for each of the periods 1960–1966 and 1967–1973 using monthly price and dividend data originally supplied by Burns Brothers and Denton Limited and as updated from the Toronto Stock Exchange *Monthly Review* and Moody's *Dividend Record*. The 65 companies consist of the overlapping set between the Burns Brothers and Denton Limited file available in July 1974 at the University of Toronto and the companies for which annual financial statement data were available for the period 1959–1973 from the files of the Financial Research Institute, with the exception of financial intermediaries and holding companies. To the extent that the data in the files were originally compiled on the basis of continuous listing on the Toronto Stock Exchange over the periods concerned and on the basis of interest to Burns Brothers and Denton Limited the sample is not a random one and is perhaps biased toward the inclusion of older, more stable companies. Nevertheless, these companies make up a significant proportion of Canadian investment holdings and consequently are of interest in their own right. Moreover, the empirical results obtained using the sample are not at variance to results using larger samples of firms listed on the New York Stock Exchange, as reported in the literature reviewed in the previous chapter.

The index of market portfolio holding-period-return relatives employed as our independent variable in estimating the market beta for each firm is the Toronto Stock Exchange Industrial Index.

The basis for its choice is its availability over the period studied, the breadth of its basis in Canadian stocks and its prominence in the minds of Canadian investors as an index of equity levels. To the extent that it is not a market value weighted index of holding-period returns on all investment assets available to investors, it falls short of the theoretical market portfolio of capital asset pricing theory. However, no such index can be observed, and it is well known that large portfolios move together very closely. Therefore we have adopted a convenient choice and assume that its use will not drastically affect our results. The fact that returns on the index do not include dividends is a minor problem, but as indicated in a recent study by Sharpe and Cooper,[11] market estimates using price relatives compare closely to those using holding-period return relatives. Note, however, that we used return relatives for each individual stock in estimating its market beta.

Turning to *independent variables*, the first to consider is the estimate of each firm's *earnings beta*. On the basis of the prior empirical studies, in particular the work by Beaver and Manegold,[12] we chose the *ex post* rate of return on common equity as the appropriate accounting income number for several reasons. Their study indicates that the number works about as well as any other in explaining market risk and it is readily obtained from the available data. It is also relatively free of time trend or size dimension and it is free of the problems encountered when earnings are deflated by market value of equity as noted in our review of Ball and Brown[13]; Beaver, Kettler and Scholes[14]; and Pettit and Westerfield,[15] presented in the previous chapter. For an index we used the total annual earnings of all the firms on the Financial Research Institute's Canann file each year divided by the total common equity of all the firms at the beginning of the year. This amounts to a size-weighted index of return on net worth for up to 400 Canadian companies and, as such, it was judged suitable for our purposes.

The *retention proportion of equity financing* variable was estimated by calculating the ratio of total retained earnings for each seven year period to the total increase in book value of common equity. Where the latter was zero or negative, the variable was set to a value of zero.

The *debt/equity* ratio was estimated by calculating the seven year average of the ratio of total debt plus preferred to total common equity plus deferred taxes, employing book values throughout for lack of market values of some debt issues.

As proxies for market expectations of *total earnings growth*, we employed three separate variables. The first is the product of the average seven-year rate of equity investment and the average rate of return on book value of common equity. In terms of earlier notation, this variable is an historical estimate of $a\bar{r}$. A second proxy is the logarithm of the ratio of common equity at the end of each seven-year period to the common equity at the beginning of the period. As such it is the historical continuous rate of growth of common equity. The third proxy was calculated in the same way, using total assets.

IV. EMPIRICAL RESULTS

Tables 7.1 and 7.2 present simple correlation results for each of the two periods 1960–1966 and 1967–1973, respectively. The mean and standard deviation for each variable are also reported there.

Tables 7.3 and 7.4 present the results of the test regressions employing the variables described above. Regression A in each table includes all of the variables except a proxy for expected earnings growth and is intended as a basis for comparison when growth proxies are added in subsequent regressions. For the period 1960–1966 the only variable in regression A with a coefficient significantly different from zero is the constant. For 1967–1973 the earnings beta has a small but significantly positive coefficient as expected and the average return on common equity variable has a significantly negative coefficient. Neither the debt/equity ratio nor the retention proportion of equity financing variable has a significant coefficient in regression A in either period. The R^2 is very low for regression A for the 1960–1966 period at 9.5 percent but it increases to 20.9 percent for 1967–1973.

Part of the poor performance of earnings beta as an explanatory variable for market beta may be a large amount of measurement error. The earnings betas were estimated using a time series

Table 7.1. Table of Simple Correlation Coefficients*, Means and Standard Deviations (1960–1966)

Variables	1	2	3	4	5	6	7	8	9	Mean	σ
1. Market Beta	1.00	.27	.36	.23	.06	.05	.32	.41	.39	.94	.30
2. Earnings Beta		1.00	.66	.46	.03	-.06	.01	.04	.26	1.08	1.82
3. Second Stage Earnings Beta**			1.00	.69	.01	-.09	.08	.15	.29	1.08	1.20
4. Debt/Equity (Book Value)				1.00	.01	-.02	.09	.12	.18	.78	.59
5. Retention Proportion of Equity Financing					1.00	.44	-.24	-.31	-.24	.75	.29
6. Average Return on Common Equity (Book Value)						1.00	.46	.33	.15	.12	.05
7. Growth Estimate for Expected Total Dividends and Earnings							1.00	.94	.67	.09	.04
8. Average Historical Growth in Total Earnings								1.00	.74	.09	.04
9. Average Historical Growth in Total Assets									1.00	.09	.05

* An absolute value greater than 0.21 indicates a positive or negative correlation at the 5 percent significance level in a one-tail test (N = 65).
** Described later in this chapter.

Table 7.2. Table of Simple Correlation Coefficients*, Means and Standard Deviations (1967–1973)

Variables	1	2	3	4	5	6	7	8	9	Mean	σ
1. Market Beta	1.00	.38	.50	-.11	.05	-.32	.01	.05	.09	1.04	.30
2. Earnings Beta		1.00	.68	-.07	-.05	-.26	-.29	-.23	-.05	.86	1.27
3. Second Stage Earnings Beta**			1.00	-.10	.22	-.39	-.38	-.35	-.19	.86	.86
4. Debt/Equity (Book Value)				1.00	-.11	.09	.30	.22	.28	.94	.81
5. Retention Proportion of Equity Financing					1.00	.11	-.22	-.21	-.14	1.21	3.31
6. Average Return on Common Equity (Book Value)						1.00	.39	.37	.33	.11	.04
7. Growth Estimate for Expected Total Dividends and Earnings							1.00	.96	.72	.08	.05
8. Average Historical Growth in Total Earnings								1.00	.77	.09	.05
9. Average Historical Growth in Total Assets									1.00	.10	.06

* An absolute value greater than 0.21 indicates a positive or negative correlation at the 5 percent significance level in a one-tail test (N = 65).
** Described later in this chapter.

rcgression on only seven annual earnings observations in each period, with the resulting low level of efficiency. One way to overcome this problem is to remove the measurement error by means of instrumental variables and this will be attempted later in the chapter. A second way is to use longer time periods with quarterly observations as well as the instrumental variable technique. This is done in the next chapter in the tests which employ U.S. data.

Returning to regression A in Tables 7.3 and 7.4, it is interesting that the debt/equity ratio doesn't have a significantly positive

Table 7.3. Market Beta vs. Contemporaneous Variables (1960–1966)

Variable	Regression Coefficients (T-values)*			
	A	B	C	D
Constant	.785	.481	.406	.566
	(6.332)	(3.394)	(2.979)	(4.143)
Earnings Beta	.035	.033	.031	.018
	(1.527)	(1.584)	(1.558)	(.813)
Debt/Equity (Book Value)	.070	.039	.031	.055
	(1.001)	(.612)	(.509)	(.842)
Retention Proportion of Equity Financing	.032	.349	.397	.193
	(.223)	(2.220)	(2.691)	(1.351)
Average Return on Common Equity (Book Value)	.323	− 2.046	− 1.845	− .488
	(.390)	(− 2.030)	(− 2.131)	(− .593)
Growth Estimate for Expected Total Dividends and Earnings (ar̄)		4.094		
		(3.566)		
Average Historical Growth in Earnings on Common			4.198	
			(4.513)	
Average Historical Growth in Total Corporate Assets				2.375
				(3.029)
R²	.095	.255	.327	.217
Standard Error	.292	.267	.254	.274
N	65	65	65	65

* A t-value greater than 1.670 in absolute value indicates a regression coefficient greater or less than zero at the 5 percent significance level in a one-tail test, assuming market betas are normally distributed.

Table 7.4. Market Beta vs. Contemporaneous Variables (1967–1973)

Variable	Regression Coefficients (T-values)*			
	A	B	C	D
Constant	1.182	1.112	1.117	1.140
	(9.968)	(9.552)	(9.622)	(9.756)
Earnings Beta	.077	.093	.088	.074
	(2.694)	(3.326)	(3.192)	(2.664)
Debt/Equity (Book Value)	− .022	− .051	− .040	− .046
	(− .511)	(− 1.197)	(− .957)	(− 1.051)
Retention Proportion of Equity Financing	.008	.016	.016	.012
	(.768)	(1.512)	(1.466)	(1.138)
Average Return on Common Equity (Book Value)	− 1.743	− 2.638	− 2.574	− 2.406
	(− 1.965)	(− 2.882)	(− 2.836)	(− 2.622)
Growth Estimate for Expected Total Dividends and Earnings (a͞r)		2.077		
		(2.594)		
Average Historical Growth in Earnings on Common			1.826	
			(2.577)	
Average Historical Growth in Total Corporate Assets				1.386
				(2.118)
R²	.209	.290	.289	.265
Standard Error	.278	.266	.266	.271
N	65	65	65	65

* A t-value greater than 1.670 in absolute value indicates a regression coefficient greater or less than zero at the 5 percent significance level in a one-tail test, assuming market betas are normally distributed.

coefficient as predicted by much of the finance literature. However, the result is consistent with our conclusion in the previous test design section where we noted that Haugen and Wichern[16] have shown that increased debt may sometimes even reduce stock risk by reducing risk that stems from stochastic capitalization rates.

The insignificant coefficients exhibited for the retention proportion of equity financing variable in regression A for each period is consistent with the theory that dividend policy has no effect on stock risk. Note that it also indicates little, if any, tendency for firms in risky lines of business to set policy in favour of lower dividends, other things equal.

The failure of the average return on common equity to take on a significant coefficient in regression A for 1960–1966, and the fact that it has a significantly negative coefficient for the 1967–1973 period, is consistent with the theory that the positive general equilibrium relationship between risk and return tends to be offset by the negative correlation between risk and return that would exist if barriers to entry are effective in reducing risk and raising average returns on equity investment.

As indicated in regression B in Tables 7.3 and 7.4, the addition of a proxy for expected earnings growth has a dramatic effect on the regression results. First, the growth variable has a significantly positive coefficient in both regressions. Second, the R^2 increases in both regressions and, interestingly, the performance of the earnings beta improves in both regressions. With the addition of a growth variable the coefficient on the average return on common equity variable becomes consistently negative in regression B for both periods and there is a significantly positive coefficient on the retention proportion of equity financing variable for the period 1960–1966. Of all these changes, the most impressive is the increase in R^2 in the regressions and the significantly positive coefficients on the growth variable. There appears to be support for our main hypothesis that growth is a factor in determining the risk of common stocks.

The use of alternate growth proxies yields similar results, as presented in regressions C and D in Tables 7.3 and 7.4. The rate of growth in total assets seems not to be as good a proxy for expected earnings growth as the other two proxies. The R^2 drops and the coefficient on the asset growth variable is reduced in size and in significance for both periods. Nevertheless, the conclusion that expected growth is an important risk variable remains unchanged.

In order to deal with the apparent problem of measurement error in the earnings beta variable, as discussed earlier, we invoked the use of instrumental variables for purposes of reducing the errors in the estimates. Table 7.5 presents the results of regressing the earnings beta estimates for each period on eleven zero-one industry variables and four other variables. The industry variables were estimated using information contained in the Toronto Stock Exchange's *Monthly Review*, in the Financial Research Institute's Canann data file and in Moody's annual publications. The debt/

Table 7.5. Earnings Betas vs. Instrumental Variables

Variables	Regression Coefficients (T-values) 1960–1966		Regression Coefficients (T-values) 1967–1973	
Constant	− 2.436	(− 2.341)	.596	(.606)
Debt/Equity (Book Value)	2.051	(4.683)	.070	(.358)
Average Return on Common Equity (Book Value)	− 2.553	(− .440)	− 2.856	(− .612)
Earnings Retention Ratio	.377	(.295)	− .687	(− .662)
Stock Financing Rate	− .072	(− .282)	− .040	(− .103)
Forest Products*	3.470	(3.461)	2.193	(3.268)
Metal Refining	2.990	(2.247)	1.001	(1.261)
Oils	2.795	(3.107)	1.065	(1.813)
Chemicals	1.932	(1.437)	.598	(.655)
Merchandise Retailers	1.892	(1.760)	.125	(.177)
Capital Goods Manufacturers	1.993	(2.187)	.757	(1.223)
Mines	1.983	(1.637)	2.446	(3.753)
Consumer Goods Manufacturers	2.208	(2.274)	.437	(.686)
Brewers and Distillers	2.306	(2.021)	.067	(.093)
Food Processors and Retailers	1.254	(1.283)	1.066	(1.740)
Pipelines	.982	(.812)	− .086	(− .106)
R^2	.435		.460	
Standard Error	1.561		1.065	
N	65		65	

* Industry variables are zero or one. The Regulated Utility industry is omitted to avoid multi-collinearity.

equity (book value) variable and the average return on common equity variable were described earlier in this chapter. The earnings retention rate and the stock financing rate were estimated by dividing total earnings for each firm in each period into the total earnings retained and the total new stock financing, respectively.

One observation on the results presented in Table 7.5 concerns the striking lack of stationarity in the regression coefficients. For example, the coefficient on the leverage variable is significantly positive, as expected, for the period 1960–1966. However, the same coefficient for 1967–1973 is close to zero and not statistically significant. The other nonindustry variables all have insignificant coefficients while most of the industry variables have positive and significant ones. This is undoubtedly due to the fact that most industries are more risky than the public utility industry which is the omitted industry variable.

In any case, the purpose of the regressions reported in Table 7.5 was to use the results in computing second stage earnings betas with reduced measurement errors. This was accomplished by subtracting the error terms of the regressions from the original earnings beta estimates and the degree of improvement in the performance of the variable can be seen in Tables 7.6 and 7.7. All but one of the second-stage earnings betas have statistically significant coefficients of the expected sign, which is a small improvement over the results in Tables 7.3 and 7.4. There is little change in the lack of significance

Table 7.6. Market Beta vs. Contemporaneous Variables (1960–1966) (With Instrumental Variable Estimates of Earnings Betas)

Variable	Regression Coefficients (T-values)*			
	A	B	C	D
Constant	.774	.490	.424	.577
	(6.397)	(3.512)	(3.107)	(4.283)
Second Stage Earnings Beta	.097	.081	.065	.063
	(2.324)	(2.087)	(1.731)	(1.529)
Debt/Equity (Book Value)	− .017	− .026	− .014	− .005
	(− .206)	(− .332)	(− .193)	(− .064)
Retention Proportion of Equity Financing	.027	.328	.373	.177
	(.199)	(2.107)	(2.522)	(1.249)
Average Return on Common Equity (Book Value)	.441	− 1.816	− 1.649	− .337
	(.543)	(− 1.808)	(− 1.879)	(− .412)
Growth Estimate for Expected Total Dividends and Earnings (a̅r̅)		3.847		
		(3.377)		
Average Historical Growth in Earnings on Common Equity			3.932	
			(4.165)	
Average Historical Growth in Total Corporate Assets				2.186
				(2.793)
R²	.137	.277	.333	.238
Standard Error	.285	.263	.253	.270
N	65	65	65	65

* A t-value greater than 1.670 in absolute value indicates a regression coefficient greater or less than zero at the 5 percent significance level in a one-tail test, assuming Market Betas are normally distributed.

Table 7.7. Market Beta vs. Contemporaneous Variables (1967–1973) (With Instrumental Variable Estimates of Earnings Betas)

Variable	Regression Coefficients (T-values)*			
	A	B	C	D
Constant	1.039	.955	.952	.987
	(8.047)	(7.586)	(7.609)	(7.827)
Second Stage Earnings Beta	.158	.182	.180	.159
	(3.592)	(4.279)	(4.270)	(3.751)
Debt/Equity (Book Value)	− .022	− .053	− .042	− .047
	(− .535)	(− 1.289)	(− 1.054)	(− 1.146)
Retention Proportion of Equity Financing	− .003	.003	.003	.001
	(− .325)	(.272)	(.275)	(.056)
Average Return on Common Equity (Book Value)	− .971	− 1.812	− 1.775	− 1.652
	(− 1.067)	(− 1.987)	(− 1.973)	(− 1.795)
Growth Estimate for Expected Total Dividends and Earnings ($\bar{ar}$)		2.133		
		(2.813)		
Average Historical Growth in Earnings on Common Equity			1.972	
			(2.933)	
Average Historical Growth in Total Corporate Assets				1.491
				(2.398)
R^2	.270	.356	.363	.335
Standard Error	.267	.253	.252	.257
N	65	65	65	65

* A t-value greater than 1.670 in absolute value indicates a regression coefficient greater or less than zero at the 5 percent significance level in a one-tail test, assuming Market Betas are normally distributed.

in the debt/equity variable and the retention proportion of equity financing is also unchanged in its performance. The coefficients on the average return on common equity are slightly less significant in value. Moreover, the effect on the outstanding performance of the growth variables has been changed very little in either direction. In summary, the use of instrumental variables has changed the regression results very little except to increase the explanatory value of the earnings beta estimates. This shows up in the greater significance of the coefficients on the second stage earnings beta and it also appears in the form of an increase in R^2 for all of the regressions in Tables 7.6 and 7.7 over those reported for the analogous regressions presented in Tables 7.3 and 7.4.

V. CONCLUSION

In concluding this chapter which has examined empirical evidence on our main hypothesis, it is fair to say that Canadian data support the theory that stock risk is a positive function of the rate at which the market expects the earnings of a firm to grow in the future. An attempt was made to design the test regressions from theoretical considerations of other risk factors to ensure, so far as possible, that the results would be a true test of the theory and that the results could not be explained by problems of specification error. It is our belief that this have been statisfactorily accomplished and that the conclusion of support for our main hypothesis, which has its foundation in analytical results, is valid.

One criticism that could possibly be leveled at the empirical work presented in this chapter is that the sample is small. While this is overcome to some extent by repeating the tests for two non-overlapping periods of time, which were quite different in many respects, a larger sample is desirable. Therefore, the following chapter is devoted to presenting the same tests using a large sample of data from U.S. firms.

Chapter VIII

A Test of the Effect of Corporate Growth on Systematic Risk: United States Data

I. INTRODUCTION

In Chapters IV and V a theoretical analysis of the market betas of common stocks produced the basis for a hypothesis that stock risk is a positive function of the rate at which total earnings and dividends are expected to grow. In Chapter VII we presented empirical evidence that supported this hypothesis for a sample of 65 Canadian stocks for two nonoverlapping periods of time, 1960–1966 and 1967–1973. The purpose of this chapter is to present additional evidence on the hypothesis based on empirical work with a larger sample of U.S. stocks. The empirical design employed here is the same as in Chapter VII. That is, the specification of the multiple regressions employed are based on the same theoretical considerations as those discussed in the test design section of the preceding chapter. However, measurement of some of the variables in the regressions is somewhat changed in an attempt to improve their performance in explaining the relative risk of the stocks concerned. These changes will be described in Section II along with a description of the overall data employed. Section III presents the empirical results, and Section IV provides a summary and conclusion.

II. U.S. DATA AND MEASUREMENT OF THE VARIABLES

The sample employed for the tests with U.S. data consisted of all firms with a complete set of required data present in the Compustat Primary Industrial File and in the S & P Industrials Index for the period 1966–1975, provided monthly closing stock prices and dividend records were also complete on the Compustat PDE file. Some firms which met these criteria were rejected for one or more of the following additional reasons:

1. There was a major merger, acquisition or discontinuance during the period, as indicated by a code in the Special Treatment Footnote field on the annual Compustat tapes,
2. The firm was a financial company, holding company, or conglomerate,
3. Cumulative earnings for the ten year period were zero or negative, or
4. Fiscal year end was a month other than December.

The first two criteria for rejection are self-explanatory. The third is required because one variable in our tests is expressed as a fraction of earnings and is therefore undefined if cumulative earnings are not positive. The fourth criteria for rejection is required in order to insure that earnings beta regressions as described below are conducted with contemporaneous earnings data. The final sample consisted of 325 firms which met all of the requirements and represents a substantial portion of the most widely traded stocks in the United States.

The variables used in the tests are listed in Table 8.1 with their intercorrelation coefficients, means and standard deviations. A description of the estimation procedure for each variable follows.

The *market beta* for each stock was estimated by regressing historical monthly market return relatives over a ten-year period on an equally weighted index of all the return relatives in the sample.

In order to obtain more efficient estimates of *earnings betas* than were used in the Canadian tests in the previous chapter, it was decided to use quarterly observations. Therefore, for the historical

Table 8.1. Table of Simple Correlation Coefficients, Means and Standard Deviations (1966–1975)

Variable	1	2	3	4	5	6	7	8	9	Mean	σ
1. Market Beta	1.00	.15	.16	.37	-.16	-.32	.04	.03	-.05	1.01	.31
2. Earnings Beta		1.00	.43	.21	-.02	.21	.40	.40	.34	.82	1.08
3. Second Stage Earnings Beta*			1.00	.49	.07	.50	.69	.64	.54	.82	.46
4. Debt/Equity (Book Value)				1.00	-.17	-.22	.11	.10	.05	.53	.48
5. Retention Proportion of Equity Financing					1.00	.14	-.07	-.06	-.09	.84	.73
6. Average Return on Common Equity (Book Value)						1.00	.66	.64	.58	.12	.06
7. Growth Estimate For Expected Total Dividends and Earnings							1.00	.96	.82	.08	.05
8. Ten-Year Growth in Total Common Equity (Book Value)								1.00	.86	.09	.06
9. Ten-Year Growth in Total Assets									1.00	.10	.06

* Described later in this chapter.

ten-year period for each firm a quarterly series of the total previous four quarter earnings divided by book value of common equity was computed. Thus each quarterly observation was an estimate of the return on book value of common equity over the previous four quarters and, as such, it abstracts from seasonal effects. Using generalized least squares to reduce inefficiency from serial correlation, each of these series was regressed on an equally weighted index of the same estimates for all 325 firms in the sample. The slope coefficients in the regressions are the earnings betas to be used in the empirical tests below.

The *debt/equity* (book value) ratio was estimated by calculating the ten-year average of the ratio of total long-term debt plus preferred equity to total common equity plus deferred taxes.

As proxies for market expectations of *total earnings growth* we calculated three separate variables. The first is the product of the average ten-year rate of equity investment as a fraction of earnings and the average rate of return on book value of common equity. In terms of earlier notation this variable is a historical estimate of $a\bar{r}$. A second proxy is the slope coefficient obtained in regressing the logarithm of book value of common equity on time and, as such, is the ordinary least squares estimate of the continuously compounded historical rate of growth in common equity. The third proxy for expected growth was calculated in the same way for each firm using total assets instead of common equity.

III. EMPIRICAL RESULTS

Table 8.2 presents the results of the test regressions employing the variables described above. The results are qualitatively similar to the Canadian tests described in the previous chapter. Regression A includes all of the variables except a proxy for expected earnings growth and is intended as a basis for comparison when growth proxies are added in regressions B, C and D.

In regression A all variables have significant coefficients except for the retention proportion of equity financing variable. Moreover, all variables have coefficient signs which are consistent with our discussion on test design in the previous chapter. The negative

Table 8.2. Market Beta vs. Contemporaneous Variables (1966–1975)

Variable	Regression Coefficients (T-values)*			
	A	B	C	D
Constant	1.104	1.098	1.117	1.092
	(23.541)	(24.009)	(24.243)	(22.900)
Earnings Beta	.046	.028	.030	.041
	(3.082)	(1.823)	(1.935)	(2.682)
Debt/Equity (Book Value)	.168	.130	.137	.162
	(4.908)	(3.772)	(3.976)	(4.695)
Retention Proportion of Equity Financing	− .029	− .013	− .016	− .024
	(− 1.374)	(− .595)	(− .770)	(− 1.106)
Average Return on Common Equity (Book Value)	− 1.606	− 2.732	− 2.537	− 1.880
	(− 5.600)	(− 7.107)	(− 6.785)	(− 5.359)
Growth Estimate for Expected Total Dividends and Earnings (ar̄)		1.901		
		(4.264)		
Ten-Year Growth in Total Common Equity (Book Value)			1.339	
			(3.774)	
Ten-Year Growth in Total Assets				.464
				(1.351)
R²	.227	.268	.260	.231
Standard Error	.274	.267	.269	.274
N	325	325	325	325

* A t-value greater than 1.65 in absolute value indicates a regression coefficient greater or less than zero at the 5 percent significance level in a one-tail test, assuming market betas are normally distributed.

coefficient on average return on common equity is consistent with barriers to entry increasing returns and reducing risk to stock investors at the same time and it indicates that this effect is empirically stronger than the positive relationship between return and risk hypothesized to exist in perfectly competitive markets. The R^2 of regression A is higher than those obtained in the previous chapter, perhaps indicating that the additional care taken to measure the variables together with the longer historical period employed has produced better results.

Upon adding a growth variable, as in regression B in Table 8.2, the coefficients which were significant in regression A remain significant with the same signs and approximate magnitudes. As with the Canadian data, the growth variable takes on a positive and very significant coefficient. Moreover, the R^2 increases by 18 percent of the value obtained in regression A. This again supports the conclusion that corporate growth is an important factor in common stock risk. The use of alternate growth variables as in regressions C and D leave the conclusion unchanged.

Failure of the growth in total assets variable to achieve a significantly positive coefficient, here as in the Canadian tests, means that it is just not as good a proxy for earnings growth as the others used, as might be expected. Another thing this reduced significance may indicate, however, is that our results are *not* due to the often alleged notion that growth shows up as a risk factor because new assets are riskier than old ones. If growth of total assets was highly correlated with the presence of a preponderance of new assets, and if new assets were riskier, then we would expect growth to be positively correlated with risk which would explain our regression results. However, if such were the case the historical growth rate of assets would be the variable most strongly correlated with risk, and that is not the case.

Here, as in the Canadian case, the earnings beta variable has taken on a relatively small coefficient and its explanatory power is also quite small, even considering that the market betas contain substantial random measurement error. In an effort to improve this performance, an attempt was again made to remove measurement error from the earnings betas through the use of instrumental variables. Table 8.3 presents the result of regressing the earnings betas on twelve zero-one industry variables and four other variables. The debt/equity (book value) and average return on common equity (book value) variables were described earlier. The earnings retention ratio is equal to total earnings retained, divided by total earnings, for the ten-year period, 1966–1975. The stock financing rate is equal to the total increase in common equity not accounted for by retained earnings divided by total earnings for the ten years. The mining industry was omitted from the industry variables to avoid multi-collinearity and therefore the coefficients on the included industry variables reflect the risk of those industries relative to mining.

Table 8.3. Earnings Betas vs. Instrumental Variables (1966–1975)

Variable	Regression Coefficients (T-values)	
Constant	− .704	(− 1.718)
Debt/Equity (Book Value)	.650	(4.140)
Average Return on Common Equity (Book Value)	5.701	(5.006)
Earnings Retention Ratio	.722	(3.018)
Stock Financing Rate	.322	(2.910)
Coal, Oil and Gas Extraction (12, 13)*	− .147	(− .292)
Construction Other than Building (16)	− .828	(− 1.353)
Food and Tobacco Processing (20, 21)	− .228	(− .587)
Textiles and Apparel (22, 23)	.298	(.679)
Lumber, Wood Products Incl. Furniture Mfg. (24, 25)	.212	(.427)
Paper Mfg., Printing, Publishing (26, 27)	.188	(.457)
Chemical Mfg., Petroleum Refining, Rubber (28–30)	.081	(.226)
Other Manufacturing (32–39)	.115	(.326)
Transportation (42, 45, 47)	− .258	(− .512)
Communication, Electric, Gas, Sanitation Utilities (48–49)	− .410	(− .857)
Wholesale Trade (50–59)	.112	(.235)
Services (70, 73, 78)	− .866	(− 1.652)
R^2	.180	
Standard Error	1.003	
N	325	

* Industry variables are zero or one. The Mining Except Fuels industry variable is omitted to avoid multicollinearity. The numbers in parentheses are the first two digits of SIC classification numbers.

Table 8.4 presents the regression results using the second stage earnings betas computed from the regression estimates presented in Table 8.3. The coefficients on the earnings beta variable have increased by a factor of five and the t-values have increased marginally. In addition, the R^2 has increased marginally for each regression in Table 8.4 relative to the analogous regression in Table 8.2. However, perhaps the most notable change is the disappearance of debt/equity as a significant variable. In every case the coefficient on debt/equity in Table 8.2 is significantly positive but in Table 8.4 the coefficients on debt/equity are not significantly different from zero. This result is probably due to the second stage earnings beta correctly reflecting the role of leverage in making earnings more

Table 8.4. Market Beta vs. Contemporaneous Variables (1966–1975) (With Instrumental Variable Estimates of Earnings Betas)

Variable	Regression Coefficients (T-values)*			
	A	B	C	D
Constant	1.140	1.118	1.140	1.131
	(24.131)	(23.784)	(24.454)	(23.213)
Second Stage Earnings Beta	.232	.129	.160	.219
	(4.275)	(2.089)	(2.738)	(3.814)
Debt/Equity (Book Value)	.053	.075	.063	.057
	(1.147)	(1.614)	(1.371)	(1.211)
Retention Proportion of Equity Financing	− .043	− .023	− .028	− .040
	(− 2.042)	(− 1.059)	(− 1.302)	(− 1.811)
Average Return on Common	− 2.546	− 3.058	− 3.038	− 2.644)
Equity (Book Value)	(− 6.567)	(− 7.395)	(− 7.318)	(− 6.452)
Growth Estimate for Expected		1.605		
Total Dividends and Earnings		(3.239)		
Ten-Year Growth in Total			1.130	
Common Equity (Book Value)			(3.061)	
Ten-Year Growth in Total Assets				.257
				(.739)
R²	.247	.271	.268	.248
Standard Error	.271	.267	.267	.271
N	325	325	325	325

* A t-value greater than 1.65 in absolute value indicates a regression coefficient greater or less than zero at the 5 percent significance level in a one-tail test, assuming market betas are normally distributed.

uncertain as a residual. The growth variable coefficients did not suffer from a similar effect to any major extent and the conclusion that expected earnings growth is a major factor in stock risk receives additional support.

IV. CONCLUSION

The purpose of this chapter was to test the theory that stock risk is a positive function of expected earnings growth using a large sample of U.S. data. A sample of 325 firms was employed in a test designed to remove confounding effects due to other factors. The regression results offer further support of the theory tested.

Chapter IX

Conclusion and Implications

In the introductory chapter of this book the declared purpose was to study the effect of corporate growth expectations on the risk of investing in common stocks, which we conceptualize as stemming from three sources: stochastic capitalization rates, stochastic long-run profitability expectations, and stochastic current period earnings. Our original intuition was that stocks of firms that are expected to grow more rapidly than average would have greater risk associated with their holding period returns, for the same reason that long-tern bonds are observed to be more volatile than are short-term bonds. In essence, the capitalization rate elasticity of stock prices should increase with expected growth just as the interest rate elasticity of bond prices increases with increased duration.

Since return on investment is most meaningful when stated relative to capitalization rates, we also hypothesized that the risk associated with unexpected changes in long-run profitability expectations would prove to be a positive function of expected corporate growth rates.

For the purpose of providing a background for the analysis, a review was conducted of dividend valuation theory and the controversy concerning the effect of dividend policy on stock risk. While the view is widely held that retention of earnings increases risk to shareholders, well-known theorems are perhaps even more widely believed to show that dividend policy is irrelevant. On the basis of our review, we conclude that neither view has been conclusively proved. However, although our main purpose was not to investigate the effects of dividend policy, per se, our analysis and empirical tests clearly support the view that dividend policy would, indeed, be irrelevant to stock valuation if markets were perfectly competitive. More precisely, in perfectly competitive capital markets, retained earnings and new equity capital appear to be perfect substitutes as sources of equity financing. To the extent that tax advantages and transaction costs favor earnings retention over new issues, the tendency should be for lower dividend payouts, and there is evidence by Brittain, reviewed in Chapter III, that such is the case. However, to the extent that dividends provide information that is not otherwise available, it may be in the interest of firms to pay higher dividends to maintain shareholder confidence in future earnings prospects. We conclude from a review of the literature on this information hypothesis that the presence of such information has yet to be established, although dividend reductions have been shown to coincide exactly with reductions in stock prices in one study. On the basis of the empirical tests reported in Chapters VII and VIII we conclude that dividend policy, per se, has no significant effect on common stock risk. The question of the effect of corporate growth, as opposed to how it is equity financed, however, is an entirely different matter.

In Chapter IV a theoretical basis was established for the theory that capitalization rate elasticity of holding period returns, and undiversifiable (systematic) holding period risk, due to stochastic capitalization rates are positive functions of the expected growth rate of total earnings. This conclusion holds whether the expected growth is from equity investment that is expected to earn positive quasi rents or not. Similarly, it was shown in Chapter V that holding period risk, both diversifiable and undiversifiable, due to stochastic long-run profitability expectations is also a positive function of expected total earnings growth. The sign of the effect of growth on systematic risk which stems from the stochastic nature of holding period earnings alone depends upon whether future returns on equity are expected to be greater than the equity capitalization rate, in which case the effect is negative, or less than the equity capitalization rate, in which case the effect of growth on stock risk is positive. However, due to the long-run nature of capitalization rate and profitability expectations, the overall effect of expected growth on stock risk is positive in sign.

The empirical tests which are reported in Chapters VII and VIII were designed after an extensive review of previous empirical work with the explicit goal of avoiding, as much as possible, spurious results that could be due to errors of specification. The only empirical tests which are capable of lending support to a theory, if it is true, are those which are capable of rejecting a testable implication if it is false. The testable implication that estimates of systematic holding period risk (market betas) are positively associated with estimates of growth expectations was not rejected under the most ideal conditions that we could apply, using both Canadian and U.S. data. Therefore, we feel that the theory that stock risk is a positive causal function of expected total earnings growth has received strong support from the data.

The implications of the theory that stock risk is a positive function of growth expectations are seriously upsetting for much of the current theory of finance. For example, one theory that is currently popular is that corporate investments can be treated as a collection of independent enterprises, provided that they are defined in such a way that their cash flows are independent. According to this theory, the sum of the net present values of the investments, if they were each treated as individual firms which are liquidated at the end of the project, is the same as the market value of the firm which undertakes the investments, but which is *not* expected to liquidate when the projects terminate one by one, ceasing to exist with the last investment. However, the theory that common stock risk is a positive function of corporate growth expectations indicates that the firm which is expected to continue undertaking additional investments, practically forever, will be a much more risky investment than the collection of individual project investments which will be liquidated upon termination of each project. Consequently, the single firm with higher long run expected earnings and dividend growth must have a higher cost of equity capital, whether from retained earnings or new issues, and its value will only equal that of the collection of terminal liquidating investments if the expected growth beyond the set of terminal investments is expected to be sufficiently profitable to compensate for the added risk presented by its very existence.

One way to give this implication more intuitive appeal is to think of two common equity investments, one of which is an investment in the collection of terminating projects alone and which will liquidate as the projects end, while the other is an investment in the same collection of terminating projects *plus* a set of options on unknown future investment projects, the value of which fluctuates widely due to changes in capitalization rates and profitability expectations. When thought of in this sense, it is clear that the investment in the set of terminating projects will be much less risky than the investment which consists of a set of identical terminating projects plus a large set of unknown options for future investment at uncertain rates of profit. This is the essence of expected corporate growth and the greater the rate of growth expected the greater is the proportion of the value of the firm which is made up of options on the future which are currently very risky investments.

The theory that greater expected growth causes greater stock risk tends to make capital budgeting a very complicated task for a firm. Whenever a pending decision on a real investment has the potential of altering investor expectations of *future* corporate growth rates it has the potential of causing a change in the risk of the firm's common stock. If a decision to invest causes investors to regard the company as having a higher growth rate objective than was previously perceived, the decision will almost certainly cause the firm's cost of equity capital to rise. Consequently, the marginal cost of capital for the investment may be very great due to its effect on the average rate at which expected future cash flows to the firm's security holders are capitalized. However, the value of the firm's stock will not fall, despite the high marginal cost of capital, provided the investment project provides a reasonable intrinsic return (which may be much lower than the marginal cost of capital) plus sufficient additional profitable growth opportunities which we characterized as unknown options for profitable future investment. Therefore, the capital budgeting decision must take into account not only the intrinsic return generated by an investment but the degree to which the investment may alter investors' expectations of future growth and the current estimate of the net present value of that expected additional growth. This latter net present value which is implicit in the capital budgeting decision must be sufficient to offset the decline in present value of existing investments when increased growth expectations result in a higher equity capitalization rate for the firm.

Notes

Chapter I

1. Robert S. Hamada, "Portfolio Analysis, Market Equilibrium and Corporate Finance," *Journal of Finance* 24 (March 1969), pp. 13–32; "The Effect of the Firm's Capital Structure on the Systematic Risk of Common Stocks," *Journal of Finance* 27 (May 1972), pp. 435–452; and "The Effects of Leverage and Corporate Taxes on the Shareholders of Public Utilities," in *Rate of Return Under Regulation: New Directions and Perspectives*, H. M. Trebing and R. H. Howard, eds., East Lansing, Michigan: Institute of Public Utilities, Michigan State University, 1969.

2. R. Richardson Pettit and Randolph Westerfield, "A Model of Capital Asset Risk," *Journal of Financial and Quantitative Analysis* 7 (March 1972), pp. 1649–1668.

3. Robert C. Merton, "An Intertemporal Capital Asset Pricing Model," *Econometrica* 41 (September 1973), pp. 867–887.

Chapter II

1. Irving N. Fisher, *The Theory of Interest* (New York: Macmillan, 1930).

2. John B. Williams, *The Theory of Investment Value* (New York: Macmillan, 1938).

3. Myron J. Gordon and Eli Shapiro, "Capital Equipment Analysis: The Required Rate of Profit," *Management Science* 3 (October 1956), pp. 102–110.

4. Merton H. Miller and Franco Modigliani, "Dividend Policy, Growth and the Valuation of Shares," *Journal of Business* 34 (October 1961), pp. 411–433.

5. Myron J. Gordon, *The Investment Financing and Valuation of the Corporation* (Homewood, Ill.: Irwin, 1962), pp. 114–123.

6. Let the total equity issue at the end of period 1 equal Q_1. Since $Q_1(1 - v)$ is the amount that accrues to the benefit of the new shares, the total dividend for the new shares at the end of period 2 is $Q_1(1 - v)r(1 - b)$. Therefore, since in efficient markets the new equity must be priced to reflect the discounted value of future dividends, we have

$$Q_1 = Q_1(1 - v)r(1 - b) \lim_{n \to \infty} \sum_{t=1}^{n} \frac{(1 + br + srv)^{t-1}}{(1 + i)^t}$$
$$= Q_1(1 - v)r(1 - b)/(i - br - srv), i > br + srv.$$

This equation may be solved for (2.12).

7. Miller and Modigliani, op. cit., p. 423.

8. Ibid., p. 421.

9. John Von Neumann and Oskar Morgenstern, *Theory of Games and Economic Behavior* (Princeton, N. J.: Princeton University Press, 1947). An elegant presentation of the theory of choice under uncertainty is Eugene F. Fama and Merton H. Miller, *The Theory of Finance* (New York: Holt, Rinehart and Winston, 1972), pp. 189–208.

10. Jack Hirschleifer, "Risk, the Discount Rate, and Investment Decision," *American Economic Review* 51 (May 1961), pp. 112–120.

11. A. H. Y. Chen, "Valuation Under Uncertainty," *Journal of Financial and Quantitative Analysis* 2 (1967), pp. 313–335.

12. Irving Fisher, op. cit.

13. John B. Williams, op. cit.

14. John C. Clendenin and Maurice Van Cleave, "Growth and Common Stock Values," *Journal of Finance* 9 (September 1954), pp. 365–376.

15. Ibid., p. 369.

16. Myron J. Gordon and Eli Shapiro, op. cit.

17. David Durand, "Growth Stocks and the Petersburg Paradox," *Journal of Finance* 12 (September 1957), pp. 348–363.

18. Daniel Bernoulli, "Exposition of a New Theory on the Measurement of Risk," *Econometrica* 22 (1954), pp. 23–26, which is a translation by Dr. Louise Sommers of Bernoulli's paper "Speciment Theoriae Novae de Mensura Sortes," *Comentarii Academiae Scientiarum Emperialis Petropolitanae* 5 (1738), pp. 175–192, as cited by Durand, op. cit.

19. Frederich R. Macauley, *Interest Rates, Bond Yields, and Stock Prices* (New York: NBER, 1938), pp. 37 ff.

20. For a test of the usefulness of the duration statistic with historical term structure data see Lawrence Fisher and Roman Weil, "Coping with the Risk of Interest Rate Fluctuations: Returns to Bondholders from Naive and Optimal Strategies," *Journal of Business* 44 (1971), pp. 408–431.

21. The duration of a growing stream of dividend expectations is

$$M_0 = \frac{\sum\limits_{t=1}^{\infty} t \cdot E_0(D_1) \cdot (1+g)^{t-1}/(1+k)^t}{\sum\limits_{t=1}^{\infty} E_0(D_1)(1+g)^{t-1}/(1+k)^t}$$

$$= \frac{\sum\limits_{t=1}^{\infty} \left[\dfrac{(1+g)^{t-1}}{(1+k)^t}\right] \cdot \left[1 + \dfrac{(1+g)}{(1+k)} + \left(\dfrac{1+g}{1+k}\right)^2 + \ldots + \left(\dfrac{1+g}{1+k}\right)^n + \ldots\right]}{\sum\limits_{t=1}^{\infty} \dfrac{(1+g)^{t-1}}{(1+k)_t}}$$

$$= \frac{1+k}{k-g}, k > g, k_1 = k_2 = \ldots = k_n = k. \tag{2.22}$$

22. Myron J. Gordon, "Dividends, Earnings, and Stock Prices," *Review of Economics and Statistics* 41 (May 1959), pp. 99–105.

23. Ibid., p. 103.

24. Merton H. Miller and Franco Modigliani, *op. cit., p.* 411–433.

25. Miller and Modigliani, op. cit., p. 421.

26. Myron J. Gordon, "Dividends, Earnings, and Stock Prices," op. cit., p. 103.

27. Myron J. Gordon, "The Savings, Investment and Valuation of a Corporation," *Review of Economics and Statistics* 44 (February 1962), pp. 37–51, Appendix A.

28. Alexander A. Robichek and Stewart C. Myers, *Optimal Financing Decisions* (Englewood Cliffs, N. J.: Prentice-Hall, 1965), pp. 79–83.

29. Chen, op. cit.

30. Robert C. Higgins, "Dividend Policy and Increasing Discount Rates: A Clarification," *Journal of Financial and Quantitative Analysis* 7 (June 1972), pp. 1757–1762.

31. John Lintner, "Optimum or Maximum Corporate Growth Under Uncertainty," in *The Corporate Economy*, ed. by Robin Marris and Adrian Wood (Cambridge, Mass.: Harvard University Press, 1971), pp. 172–241.

Chapter III

1. John Lintner, "Distribution of Incomes of Corporations Among Dividends, Retained Earnings, and Taxes," *American Economic Review* 46 (May 1956), pp. 97–113.

2. The original partial adjustment model proposed by Lintner, op. cit., contained a constant term, α, to reflect the reluctance of management to reduce dividends. However, such a constant term would cause dividends to asymptotically approach $qY_t + \alpha$ which is not consistent with the definition of q as a target payout fraction. As we will see, much empirical work supports (3.2) without the constant.

3. S. J. Prais, "Dividend Policy and Income Appropriation," in *Studies in Company Finance*, B. Tew and R. F. Henderson, eds., (Cambridge, Mass.: Cambridge University Press, 1959).

4. Milton Friedman, *A Theory of the Consumption Function* (Princeton, N. J.: Princeton University Press, 1957).

5. Roger N. Waud, "Small Sample Bias Due to Misspecification in the 'Partial Adjustment' and 'Adaptive Expectations' Models," *American Statistical Association Journal* 61(1966), pp. 1130–1152.

6. Lintner, op. cit.; Paul G. Darling, "The Influence of Expectations and Liquidity on Dividend Policy," *Journal of Political Economy* (1957), pp. 209–224; John A. Brittain, *Corporate Dividend Policy* (Washington, D.C.: Brookings Institution, 1966).

7. Eugene F. Fama and Harvey Babiak, "Dividend Policy: An Empirical Analysis," *Journal of the American Statistical Association* 63(1968), pp. 1132–1161; Jean-Pierre Chateau, "A Microeconometric Study of Canadian Corporate Dividend Policy," *Proceedings of the First Annual Meeting of the European Finance Association*, Amsterdam: North Holland, pp. 281–310; and "Dividend Policy Revisited: Within- and Out-of-Sample Tests," W. P. 76–43, Faculty of Management, McGill University.

8. Op. cit.

9. Op. cit.

10. Britain, 1966, op. cit.

11. Ibid., p. 53.

12. Ibid., p. 56.

13. Op. cit.

14. Op. cit.

15. Op. cit.

16. Op. cit., pp. 1133–1134.

17. Fama and Babiak conclude incorrectly that the adaptive expectations model is inappropriate.

18. Op. cit.

19. C. Hildreth and J. Y. Lu, "Demand Relations with Autocorrelated Disturbances," Agricultural Experimental Station, Michigan State University, Tech. Bul. 276, cited by Chateau, op. cit.

20. M. S. Feldstein, "Corporate Taxation and Dividend Behavior," *Review of Economic Studies* 37(1970), pp. 57–72.

21. Chateau, op. cit.

22. Op. cit.

23. Edwin Kuh, *Capital Stock Growth: A Micro-Econometric Approach* (Amsterdam: North Holland, 1971), pp. 37–38.

24. Op. cit.

25. Op. cit.

26. Op. cit.

27. Franco Modigliani and Merton Miller, "The Cost of Capital, Corporation Finance, and the Theory of Investment: Reply," *American Economic Review* 49 (1959), pp. 655–669; Merton H. Miller and Franco Modigliani, "Dividend Policy, Growth, and the Valuation of Shares," *Journal of Business* 34 (1961), pp. 411–433; and "Some Estimates of the Cost of Capital to the Electric Utility Industry, 1954–57," *American Economic Review* 56(1966).

28. R. Richardson Pettit, "Dividend Announcements, Security Performance, and Capital Market Efficiency," *Journal of Finance* 27 (1972), pp. 993–1007.

29. E. Fama, L. Fisher, M. C. Jensen, and R. Roll, "The Adjustment of Stock Prices to New Information," *International Economic Review*, (1969), pp. 1–26.

30. R. Watts, "The Information Content of Dividends," *Journal of Business* 46 (1973), pp. 191–211.

31. Op. cit.

32. Op. cit.

33. James S. Ang, "Dividend Policy: Informational Content or Partial Adjustment," *Review of Economics and Statistics* 57 (1975), pp. 65–70; and P. Michael Laub, "On the Informational Content of Dividends," *Journal of Business* 49 (1976), pp. 73–80.

34. Op. cit.

35. Op. cit.

36. Op. cit.

37. Op. cit.

Chapter IV

1. Op. cit.

2. Myron J. Gordon, *The Investment Financing and Valuation of the Corporation.*

3. David R. Fewings, "The Impact of Corporate Growth on the Risk of Common Stocks," *Journal of Finance* 30 (May 1975), pp. 525–531.

4. Op. cit.

5. Op. cit.

6. For the original derivation of this statistic see, J. R. Hicks, *Value and Capital*, 2nd ed. (Oxford University Press, 1946): pp. 184–188.

7. Lawrence Fisher and Roman Weil, op. cit.

8. Merton H. Miller and Franco Modigliani, op. cit., and Myron J. Gordon, *The Investment, Financing and Valuation of the Corporation*. Recall that b and s are the rates of earnings retention and new stock financing, respectively, as a fraction of earnings, while r is the rate of return on net worth and k_0 is the capitalization rate.

9. A failure to realize that the growth rate of dividends is a function of the capitalization rate has plagued the work of others as well. See Edwin P. Mampe, Jr., "The Impact of Interest Rates on Share Prices: The Influence of Expectations, Growth and Leverage" (unpublished Ph.D. dissertation, University of Illinois, 1968); Robert A. Haugen, "Expected Growth, Required Return, and the Variability of Stock Prices" *Journal of Financial and Quantitative Analysis* 5 (September 1970), pp. 297–307; John Lintner, op. cit.; and Robert A. Haugen and Dean W. Wichern, "The Elasticity of Financial Assets," *Journal of Finance* 29 (September 1974), pp. 1229–1240.

10. See for example Burton G. Malkiel, *The Term Structure of Interest Rates* (Princeton, N. J.: Princeton University Press, 1966), pp. 8 and 67–68.

11. Harry Markowitz, *Portfolio Selection* (New Haven and London: Yale University Press, Cowles Foundation Monograph, 1959).

12. William F. Sharpe, "Capital Asset Prices: A Theory of Market Equilibrium Under Conditions of Risk," *Journal of Finance* 19 (September 1964), pp. 425–442.

13. John Lintner, "The Valuation of Risk Assets and the Selection of Risky Investments in Stock Portfolios and Capital Budgets," *Review of Economics and Statistics* 47 (February 1965), pp. 13–37.

14. An asset with holding-period return having zero covariance with the return on a market-value-weighted portfolio of assets which are positively covaried in their returns.

15. E. R. Fama and J. D. MacBeth, "Risk, Return and Equilibrium: Empirical Tests," *Journal of Political Economy* (1973), pp. 607–636.

16. Richard E. Johnson and Fred L. Kiekemeister, *Calculus*, 2nd ed. (Boston: Allyn and Bacon, 1960), pp. 560–561.

Chapter V

1. Op. cit.

2. Myron J. Gordon, *The Investment Financing and Valuation of the Corporation*.

3. Let the total equity issue at the end of period t equal Q. Since $Q_t(1 - v_t)$ of the issue accrues to the benefit of new shares the total dividend of the new shares at the end of period $t + 1$ is expected to be $Q_t(1 - v_t)\bar{r}_t(1 - b)$. In efficient markets the new equity issue will be priced to reflect the discounted value of future expected dividends which grow at the rate $b\bar{r}_t + s\bar{r}_t v_t$. Therefore

$$Q_t = Q_t(1 - v_t)\bar{r}_t(1 - b) \lim_{n \to \infty} \sum_{j=1}^{n} \frac{(1 + b\bar{r}_t + s\bar{r}_t v_t)^{j-1}}{(1 + k_t)^j}$$

$$= \frac{Q_t(1 - v_t)\bar{r}_t(1 - b)}{i - b\bar{r}_t - s\bar{r}_t v_t}, \quad b\bar{r}_t + s\bar{r}_t v_t < i.$$

Solving for v_t yields equation (5.11).

4. John Lintner, "Distribution of Incomes of Corporations Among Dividends, Retained Earnings and Taxes," *American Economic Review* 46 (May 1956), pp. 97–113.

5. See Chapter 2, Section II, for a comparison of equation (3.3) and (3.6).

6. Myron J. Gordon, *The Investment, Financing and Valuation of the Corporation*, pp. 119–123; and *The Cost of Capital to a Public Utility* (East Lansing, Mich.: MSU Public Utilities Studies, 1974), pp. 30–33.

Chapter VI

1. Ray Ball and Philip Brown, "Portfolio Theory and Accounting," *Journal of Accounting Research* (Autumn 1969), pp. 300–323.

2. William Beaver, Paul Kettler and Myron Scholes, "The Association Between Market Determined and Accounting Determined Risk Measures," *The Accounting Review* (October 1970), pp. 654–682.

3. Myron J. Gordon and Paul Halpern, "Cost of Capital for a Division of a Firm," *Journal of Finance* 29 (September 1974), pp. 1153–1163.

4. Op. cit.

5. Op. cit.

6. J. Johnston, *Econometric Methods*, 2nd ed. (New York: McGraw-Hill, 1960), pp. 228–238.

7. Y. Haitovsky, "Unbiased Multiple Regression Coefficients Estimated from One-Way-Classification Tables when the Cross Classifications Are Unknown," *Journal of the American Statistical Association* 61 (1966), pp. 720–728, as cited by Johnston, ibid.

8. G. H. Orcutt, H. W. Watts, and J. B. Edwards, "Data Aggregation and Information Loss," *American Economic Review* (September 1968), as cited by Johnston, op. cit.

9. J. S. Cramer, "Efficient Grouping, Regression and Correlation in Engel Curve Analysis," *Journal of the American Statistical Association* 59 (1964), pp. 233–250, as cited by Johnston, op. cit.

10. Myron J. Gordon, "Optimal Investment and Financing Policy," *Journal of Finance* (May 1963), p. 267.

11. Richardson R. Pettit and Randolph Westerfield, op. cit.

12. Myron J. Gordon, *The Cost of Capital to a Public Utility*, pp. 125–28.

13. Dennis E. Logue and Larry J. Merville, "Financial Policy and Market Expectations," *Financial Management* (Summer 1972), pp. 37–44.

14. Myron J. Gordon and Paul J. Halpern, "Cost of Capital for a Division of a Firm," *Journal of Finance* 29 (September 1974), pp. 1153–1163.

15. Henry Theil, *Principles of Econometrics* (Wiley, 1971), p. 254.

16. Nicholas J. Gonedes, "Evidence on the Information Content of Accounting Numbers: Accounting-Based and Market-Based Estimates of Systematic Risk," *Journal of Financial and Quantitative Analysis* 8 (June 1973), pp. 407–443; and "A Note on Accounting Based and Market-Based Estimates of Systematic Risk," *Journal of Financial and Quantitative Analysis* 10 (June 1975), pp. 355–365.

17. William Beaver and James Manegold, "The Association Between Market-Determined and Accounting-Determined Measures of Systematic Risk: Some Further Evidence," *Journal of Financial and Quantitative Analysis* 10 (June 1975), pp. 231–284..

18. Barr Rosenberg and Walt McKibben, "The Prediction of Systematic and Specific Risk in Common Stocks," *Journal of Financial and Quantitative Analysis* 8 (March 1973), pp. 317–333; William J. Breen and Eugene M. Lerner, "Corporate Financial Strategies and Market Measures of Risk and Return," *Journal of Finance* 28 (May 1973), pp. 339–351; and Ronald W. Melicher, "Financial Factors Which Influence Beta Variations Within an Homogeneous Industry Environment," *Journal of Financial and Quantitative Analysis* 9 (March 1974), p. 231.

Chapter VII

1. Franco Modigliani and Merton Miller, "The Cost of Capital, Corporation Finance and the Theory of Investment," *American Economic Review* 48 (June 1958), pp. 261–297; and "Taxes and the Cost of Capital: A Correction," *American Economic Review* 53 (June 1963), pp. 433–443.

2. Robert S. Hamada, "Portfolio Analysis, Market Equilibrium and Corporation Finance," *Journal of Finance* 24 (March 1969), pp. 13–32.

3. Robert A Haugen and Dean W. Wichern, "The Intricate Relationship Between Financial Leverage and the Stability of Stock Prices," *Journal of Finance* 5, XXX, pp. 1283–1292.

4. Eugene F. Fama, "Efficient Capital Markets: A Review of Theory and Empirical Work," *Journal of Finance* 25 (May 1970), pp. 383–417.

5. William F. Sharpe and Guy M. Cooper, "Risk-Return Classes of New York Stock Exchange Common Stocks, 1931–67," *Financial Analysts Journal* 28 (March, April 1972).

6. Marshall E. Blume, "On the Assessment of Risk," *Journal of Finance* 26 (March 1971), pp. 1–10.

7. Nicholas J. Gonedes, "Evidence on the Information Content of Accounting Numbers: Accounting-Based and Market-Based Estimates of Systematic Risk," *Journal of Financial and Quantitative Analysis* 8 (June 1973), pp. 407–443.

8. Eugene F. Fama, "The Behavior of Stock Prices," *Journal of Business* 38 (July 1965), pp. 34–105; and Eugene F. Fama and James MacBeth, "Risk, Return and Equilibrium: Empirical Tests," *Journal of Policical Economy* 81 (May–June 1973).

9. S. J. Press, "A Compound Events Model of Security Prices," *Journal of Business* 41 (July 1968), pp. 317–335; P. D. Praetz, "The Distribution of Share Price Changes," *Journal of Business* 45 (January 1972), pp. 49–55; and Robert C. Blattberg and Nicholas J. Gonedes,"A Comparison of the Stable and Student Distributions as Statistical Models for Stock Prices," *Journal of Business* 47 (April 1974), pp. 244–280.

10. Op. cit.
11. Op. cit.
12. Op. cit.
13. Op. cit.
14. Op. cit.
15. Op. cit.
16. Op. cit.

Index